THIS BOOK
BELONGS TO

....

Did you like my book? I pondered it severely before releasing this book. Although the response has been overwhelming, it is always pleasing to see, read or hear a new comment. Thank you for reading this and I would love to hear your honest opinion about it. Furthermore, many people are searching for a unique book, and your feedback will help me gather the right books for my reading audience.

Thanks!

©COPYRIGHT 2023
ALL RIGHTS RESERVED

The content contained within this book may not be reproduced, duplicated, or transmitted without direct written permission from the author or the publisher. Under no circumstances will any blame or legal responsibility be held against the publisher, or author, for any damages, reparation, or monetary loss due to the information contained within this book. Either directly or indirectly.

Legal Notice:
This book is copyright protected. This book is only for personal use. You cannot amend, distribute, sell, use, quote, or paraphrase any part, or the content within this book, without the consent of the author or publisher.

Disclaimer Notice:
Please note the information contained within this document is for educational and entertainment purposes only. All effort has been executed to present accurate, up-to-date, and reliable, complete information. No warranties of any kind are declared or implied. Readers acknowledge that the author is not engaging in the rendering of legal, financial, medical, or professional advice. The content within this book has been derived from various sources. Please consult a licensed professional before attempting any techniques outlined in this book. By reading this document, the reader agrees that under no circumstances is the author responsible for any losses, direct or indirect, which are incurred as a result of the use of the information contained within this document, including, but not limited to — errors, omissions, or inaccuracies.

Table of Contents

SUMMARY	1
Hat Selector	25
Knit Patterns	27
Dinosaur	27
Bobble Hat	34
Strawberry	38
Pumpkin	43
Sports Cap	48
Spring Chick	50
Punk Mohawk	54
Bunny	61
Turkey	65
Flower Cap	70
I Heart You	74
Extraterrestrial	77
Reindeer Antlers	82
Party Hat	86
Witch	90
Cupcake	94
Banana	97
Santa Hat	102
Elf	106
Top Hat	111
Crochet Patterns	115
Pom Pom Hat	115
Little Lion	120
Feline Fox	125
Baby Bear	132
Dog	138
Shark Attack	146
Santa Paws	153
Candy Corn	161

Unicorn	170
Cowboy Hat	176
Techniques	181
Materials and Equipment	182
Knitting Techniques	186
Crochet Techniques	191
Additional Techniques	195
Abbreviations	199
Reading Charts	200
Yarns Used	202

SUMMARY

The Joy of Crafting for Your Furry Friends (Cat): Crafting for your furry friends, especially cats, can bring immense joy and satisfaction. Not only does it provide a creative outlet for you, but it also allows you to create personalized and unique items for your beloved feline companion. From toys and beds to scratching posts and feeding stations, the possibilities are endless when it comes to crafting for your cat.

One of the most popular crafts for cats is making homemade toys. Cats are natural hunters, and providing them with interactive toys can help stimulate their instincts and keep them entertained. You can easily create toys using materials such as felt, feathers, and catnip. For example, you can sew a small pouch filled with catnip and feathers, creating a toy that will entice your cat to play and pounce. Additionally, you can make a wand toy by attaching feathers or a small plush toy to a stick or dowel. This interactive toy will provide hours of fun for both you and your cat.

Another craft that can bring joy to your furry friend is creating a cozy and comfortable bed. Cats love to curl up and sleep in warm and snug spaces, so why not make them a bed that they will adore? You can use soft fabrics such as fleece or plush to sew a simple bed, or you can repurpose an old sweater or blanket to create a unique and personalized sleeping spot for your cat. Adding a cushion or stuffing to the bed will provide extra comfort, ensuring that your cat has a restful sleep.

Scratching is a natural behavior for cats, and providing them with a designated scratching post can save your furniture from their sharp claws. Crafting a scratching post can be a fun and rewarding project.

You can use materials such as sisal rope or carpet to cover a sturdy base, creating a surface that your cat will love to scratch. Adding a small platform or perch on top of the scratching post will give your cat a place to relax and observe their surroundings.

Crafting for your cat can also extend to their feeding station. You can create a personalized food and water bowl set by painting or decorating plain ceramic bowls. Adding your cat's name or a cute design will make mealtime feel special for your furry friend. Additionally, you can make a raised feeding station by repurposing old wooden crates or boxes. Elevating the bowls will make it more comfortable for your cat to eat and drink, reducing strain on their neck and spine.

In conclusion, crafting for your furry friend, specifically cats, can bring immense joy and satisfaction.

Exploring the World of Cat Fashion in Crochet Hat Patterns for Your Cat: Are you a cat lover who enjoys dressing up your feline friend in adorable and fashionable accessories? If so, then you're in for a treat! In this article, we will be delving into the fascinating world of cat fashion, specifically focusing on crochet hat patterns for your beloved cat.

Crochet has become increasingly popular in recent years, with enthusiasts creating a wide range of items, from clothing to home decor. And now, cat owners have jumped on the crochet bandwagon, creating stylish and unique hats for their furry companions.

One of the reasons why crochet hats for cats have gained popularity is the sheer cuteness factor. Seeing a cat donning a tiny hat can melt even the coldest of hearts. These hats come in various designs, ranging from simple and elegant to whimsical and fun. Whether you prefer a classic beanie style or a quirky animal-themed hat, there is a crochet pattern out there to suit every cat's personality.

But cat fashion isn't just about aesthetics; it can also serve a practical purpose. Crochet hats can help keep your cat warm during colder months or protect them from the sun's harmful rays during the summer. Additionally, some cats may have medical conditions that require them to wear hats for protection or to cover wounds. Crochet hats provide a comfortable and stylish solution to these needs.

Now, let's talk about the different types of crochet hat patterns available for your cat. The most common style is the beanie, which is a simple and versatile design that can be customized with various colors and embellishments. This style is perfect for everyday wear and can be easily adjusted to fit your cat's head size.

If you're looking to add a touch of whimsy to your cat's wardrobe, animal-themed crochet hats are a great choice. From adorable bunny ears to fierce lion manes, these hats are sure to make your cat the center of attention wherever they go. These patterns often include additional elements like tails or paws, adding an extra level of cuteness to the overall look.

For those who prefer a more elegant and sophisticated style, there are crochet hat patterns that mimic the look of traditional human hats. From fedoras to berets, these designs add a touch of class to your cat's ensemble. These hats are perfect for special occasions or for those cats who prefer a more refined look.

Now that you're familiar with the world of cat fashion in crochet hat patterns, you may be wondering how to get started.

Crochet Hat for Your Cat, Ensuring Comfort and Safety in Cat Wearables: Introducing the Crochet Hat for Your Cat, a stylish and adorable accessory that not only adds a touch of cuteness to your feline friend but also ensures their comfort and safety in cat wearables.

We understand that as a cat owner, you want to provide the best for your beloved pet. That's why our crochet hat is meticulously designed with their well-being in mind. Made from soft and breathable materials, it guarantees a comfortable fit for your cat, allowing them to move freely without any discomfort.

Safety is our top priority, and we have taken every precaution to ensure that our crochet hat is completely safe for your cat to wear. The hat is securely fastened with adjustable straps, preventing it from slipping off or causing any harm to your pet. The straps are also designed to be gentle on your cat's delicate skin, avoiding any irritation or discomfort.

Additionally, our crochet hat is lightweight, so your cat won't feel burdened or restricted while wearing it. Cats are known for their independent nature, and we have taken this into consideration when designing our hat. It allows your cat to maintain their natural agility and freedom of movement, ensuring they can still climb, jump, and play without any hindrance.

Not only is our crochet hat functional and safe, but it also adds a touch of style to your cat's wardrobe. Available in a variety of colors and patterns, you can choose the perfect hat to match your cat's personality and showcase their unique style. Whether you prefer a vibrant and playful design or a more subtle and elegant look, we have options to suit every taste.

Furthermore, our crochet hat is easy to clean and maintain. Simply hand wash it with mild detergent and let it air dry, and it will be ready for your cat to wear again in no time. The durable construction ensures that the hat will withstand regular use and maintain its shape and quality over time.

In conclusion, the Crochet Hat for Your Cat is the perfect accessory to enhance your cat's style while prioritizing their comfort and safety. With its soft and breathable materials, secure fastening, lightweight design, and stylish options, it is a must-have for any cat owner who wants to provide their pet with the best. So why wait? Treat your furry friend to a crochet hat and watch them strut their stuff with confidence and charm.

Using This Book to Create Adorable Feline in Crochet Hat Patterns for Your Cat: This book is a comprehensive guide that will help you create the most adorable feline crochet hat patterns for your beloved cat. Whether you are a beginner or an experienced crocheter, this book is designed to cater to all skill levels and provide you with step-by-step instructions to create unique and stylish hats for your furry friend.

The book starts off by introducing you to the world of crochet and familiarizing you with the basic techniques and stitches required to complete the patterns. It provides clear and concise explanations, accompanied by detailed illustrations, making it easy for even a novice to follow along.

Once you have mastered the basics, the book dives into the exciting world of feline crochet hat patterns. It offers a wide range of designs, from simple and classic styles to more intricate and whimsical creations. Each pattern is carefully crafted to ensure a comfortable fit for your cat, taking into consideration their size and unique features.

The book also includes tips and tricks to customize the hats according to your cat's personality and preferences. Whether your cat is playful and energetic or calm and reserved, you can easily adapt the patterns to reflect their individuality. Additionally, the book provides guidance on choosing the right yarn and colors to create visually appealing hats that will make your cat the center of attention.

What sets this book apart is its attention to detail and emphasis on creating hats that are not only cute but also functional. The patterns are designed to provide warmth and protection for your cat, especially during colder months or when venturing outdoors. The book includes instructions on adding ear flaps, chin straps, and other features to ensure a secure and comfortable fit.

Furthermore, the book offers inspiration and ideas for incorporating additional embellishments and accessories to enhance the hats. From bows and flowers to pom-poms and buttons, you can easily personalize the hats to match your cat's style and make them truly unique.

In addition to the patterns, the book also provides valuable information on caring for the hats and ensuring their longevity. It offers tips on washing, storing, and repairing the hats, so you can enjoy them for years to come.

Overall, Using This Book to Create Adorable Feline in Crochet Hat Patterns for Your Cat is a must-have resource for any cat lover who wants to indulge in their passion for crochet and create stylish and comfortable hats for their furry companions.

Understanding Yarns, Needles, and Hooks in Crochet Hat for Your Cat: When it comes to crocheting a hat for your cat, it's important to have a good understanding of the different materials and tools involved. Yarns, needles, and hooks all play a crucial role in creating a comfortable and stylish hat that your feline friend will love.

First and foremost, let's talk about yarns. Choosing the right yarn for your cat's hat is essential for both comfort and durability. Cats have sensitive skin, so it's important to select a soft and non-irritating yarn. Acrylic yarns are a popular choice for cat hats as they are soft, easy to care for, and come in a wide range of colors. However, if you prefer natural fibers, you can opt for cotton or bamboo yarns, which are also gentle on your cat's skin.

Next, let's discuss needles. The size of the needles you use will depend on the thickness of the yarn you've chosen. Thicker yarns require larger needles, while thinner yarns call for smaller ones. It's important to choose the right needle size to achieve the desired tension and stitch definition in your cat's hat. Additionally, consider using circular needles instead of straight ones, as they allow you to easily work in the round and create a seamless hat.

Lastly, let's delve into hooks. Crochet hooks come in various sizes, and just like needles, the size you choose should correspond to the thickness of your yarn. Hooks with smaller sizes are suitable for finer yarns, while larger hooks are better for bulkier yarns. Additionally, the type of hook you use can also affect the outcome of your cat's hat. Traditional hooks with a tapered throat are great for beginners, while ergonomic hooks with a comfortable grip can reduce hand fatigue during longer crochet sessions.

In conclusion, understanding the different yarns, needles, and hooks used in crocheting a hat for your cat is crucial for a successful and enjoyable project. By selecting the right materials and tools, you can create a hat that not only looks adorable on your feline companion but also provides them with the comfort they deserve. So, take your time to explore different yarn options, choose the appropriate needle size, and find a hook that feels comfortable in your hand. With a little practice and patience, you'll be able to crochet a hat that your cat will proudly wear.

Ensuring Feline Comfort and Safety in Wearables of Crochet Hat for Your Cat: When it comes to ensuring the comfort and safety of your feline friend, it is important to consider every aspect of their well-being, even when it comes to fashion choices such as crochet hats. While it may seem like a fun and adorable accessory for your cat, it is crucial to prioritize their comfort and safety above all else.

First and foremost, it is essential to choose the right size and fit for your cat's crochet hat. Just like humans, cats come in different shapes and sizes, so it is important to measure your cat's head circumference accurately before purchasing or making a hat. A hat that is too tight can cause discomfort and restrict their movement, while a hat that is too loose may fall off easily and pose a choking hazard. Ensuring a snug yet comfortable fit is key to keeping your cat happy and safe while wearing a crochet hat.

Additionally, the choice of materials used in the crochet hat is crucial for your cat's comfort. Opt for soft and breathable yarns that will not irritate their skin or cause any allergic reactions. Avoid using materials that shed easily, as loose fibers can be ingested by your cat and lead to digestive issues. It is also important to consider the weight of the hat, as a heavy hat can cause discomfort and strain on your cat's neck.

Furthermore, it is important to consider the design and construction of the crochet hat. Avoid using any small or dangling embellishments that your cat could potentially chew on or swallow. These can pose a choking hazard and should be avoided at all costs. Instead, opt for a simple and secure design that will stay in place without causing any discomfort or harm to your cat.

When introducing your cat to wearing a crochet hat, it is crucial to do so gradually and with patience. Cats are naturally independent creatures and may not take kindly to having something placed on their heads. Start by allowing your cat to sniff and explore the hat before gently placing it on their head for short periods of time. Reward them with treats and praise to create positive associations with wearing the hat. If your cat shows signs of distress or discomfort, remove the hat immediately and try again at a later time.

Lastly, it is important to always supervise your cat while they are wearing a crochet hat. While it may be tempting to leave them unattended, accidents can happen, and it is crucial to be there to intervene if necessary.

Measuring Your Cat for a Perfect Fit in Crochet Hat for Your Cat: When it comes to crocheting a hat for your cat, ensuring a perfect fit is essential. Just like humans, cats come in different shapes and sizes, so taking accurate measurements is crucial to create a hat that your feline friend will feel comfortable wearing.

To begin, gather the necessary tools for measuring your cat. You will need a flexible measuring tape, a pen or pencil, and a piece of paper to record the measurements. It's also helpful to have some treats or toys nearby to keep your cat engaged and cooperative during the process.

Start by measuring the circumference of your cat's head. Place the measuring tape around the widest part of their head, just above the ears and eyebrows. Make sure the tape is snug but not too tight, as you want the hat to fit comfortably. Take note of this measurement, as it will be the basis for determining the size of the hat.

Next, measure the distance from the base of your cat's ear to the top of their head. This measurement will help you determine the height of the hat. Gently hold your cat's ear down and place the measuring tape at the base, then extend it vertically to the top of their head. Again, record this measurement for reference.

Now, it's time to measure the distance from the base of one ear to the base of the other. This measurement will help you determine the width of the hat. Place the measuring tape at the base of one ear and extend it across the top of your cat's head to the base of the other ear. Be sure to keep the tape straight and level. Write down this measurement as well.

Additionally, you may want to measure the length of your cat's neck. This measurement can be helpful if you plan to incorporate a strap or tie to secure the hat in place. Place the measuring tape around the base of your cat's neck, just below their chin, and record the measurement.

Once you have all the necessary measurements, you can use them as a guide to crochet a hat that fits your cat perfectly. Keep in mind that crochet patterns often provide size guidelines, so compare your measurements to the pattern's recommendations to ensure the best fit.

Remember, cats can be sensitive to wearing accessories, so it's important to introduce the hat gradually and monitor your cat's comfort level. If your cat shows any signs of distress or discomfort, it may be necessary to adjust the hat or consider alternative options.

Basic Stitches and Techniques for Beginners in Crochet Hat for Your Cat: Crocheting a hat for your cat can be a fun and rewarding project, especially if you are a beginner in crochet. To get started, it's important to familiarize yourself with some basic stitches and techniques that will help you create a cozy and stylish hat for your feline friend.

One of the most commonly used stitches in crochet is the chain stitch. This stitch forms the foundation of your project and is used to create a starting row. To make a chain stitch, simply yarn over and pull the yarn through the loop on your hook. Repeat this process until you have the desired number of chains for your hat.

Once you have your chain stitches, you can move on to the single crochet stitch. This stitch is used to create a tight and sturdy fabric, perfect for keeping your cat's head warm. To make a single crochet stitch, insert your hook into the next chain stitch, yarn over, and pull the yarn through the chain stitch. Yarn over again and pull through both loops on your hook. Repeat this process for each chain stitch until you reach the end of the row.

To shape the hat, you can also use increases and decreases. Increases are used to add stitches and create a wider circumference, while decreases are used to reduce stitches and create a tapered shape. One common increase stitch is the double crochet increase. To make this stitch, yarn over, insert your hook into the next stitch, yarn over again, and pull through the stitch. Yarn over once more and pull through the first two loops on your hook. Yarn over again and pull through the remaining two loops. Repeat this process for each stitch you want to increase.

For decreases, you can use the single crochet decrease stitch. To make this stitch, insert your hook into the next stitch, yarn over and pull through the stitch. Insert your hook into the next stitch, yarn over and pull through the stitch. Yarn over again and pull through all three loops on your hook. Repeat this process for each stitch you want to decrease.

In addition to these basic stitches, you can also experiment with different crochet techniques to add texture and design elements to your cat's hat. For example, you can try the popcorn stitch, which creates a raised, bumpy texture. To make a popcorn stitch, work several double crochet stitches into the same stitch, but do not complete the final step of each stitch.

Ensuring Durability and Longevity in Handmade Items in Crochet Hat for Your Cat: When it comes to handmade items, durability and longevity are key factors that every consumer looks for. This is especially true when it comes to crochet hats for your beloved feline friend. As a pet owner, you want to ensure that the hat you purchase for your cat not only looks adorable but also stands the test of time.

Crochet hats for cats are not just a fashion statement, but also serve a practical purpose. They provide warmth and protection for your cat's ears during colder months or in chilly environments. Therefore, it is essential to choose a hat that is not only aesthetically pleasing but also made to last.

One of the primary factors that contribute to the durability of a crochet hat is the quality of materials used. Opting for high-quality yarns that are known for their strength and durability is crucial. Look for yarns that are made from natural fibers such as cotton or wool, as they tend to be more resilient and less prone to wear and tear. Additionally, consider the thickness of the yarn, as thicker yarns are generally more durable than thinner ones.

Another aspect to consider is the construction of the hat. Handmade crochet hats that are carefully crafted with attention to detail are more likely to withstand the test of time. Look for hats that have reinforced stitching, especially in areas that are prone to stretching or tearing, such as the brim or ear holes. This will ensure that the hat remains intact even with regular use.

Furthermore, the size and fit of the hat are crucial for its longevity. A hat that is too tight may cause discomfort for your cat and increase the likelihood of it being damaged or torn. On the other hand, a hat that is too loose may easily slip off or get caught on objects, leading to potential damage. Therefore, it is important to choose a hat that fits your cat snugly but comfortably, allowing for ease of movement without compromising its durability.

Proper care and maintenance also play a significant role in ensuring the longevity of a crochet hat. While cats are known for their grooming habits, it is still important to regularly inspect the hat for any signs of damage or wear. If any loose threads or stitches are found, it is best to repair them promptly to prevent further damage. Additionally, washing the hat according to the manufacturer's instructions, or handwashing it with mild detergent, will help maintain its shape and integrity.

Guide: Washing and Cleaning Knit and Crochet Hats:

Introduction:

Knit and crochet hats are not only fashionable but also provide warmth and comfort during the colder months. However, over time, these hats can accumulate dirt, sweat, and odors, making it necessary to clean them regularly. In this guide, we will provide you with detailed instructions on how to properly wash and clean your knit and crochet hats, ensuring that they remain in excellent condition for years to come.

Materials Needed:

Before we dive into the cleaning process, let's gather the materials you will need:

1. Mild detergent or baby shampoo: Opt for a gentle detergent that won't damage the delicate fibers of your hat.

2. Soft-bristled brush: This will help remove any stubborn stains or dirt particles.

3. Clean towels: These will be used for drying your hat.

4. Mesh laundry bag: This optional item will protect your hat from getting tangled or stretched during the washing machine cycle.

5. Hat form or towel: This will help maintain the shape of your hat while it dries.

Step 1: Spot Cleaning:

Before washing your entire hat, it's essential to spot clean any visible stains or dirt. To do this, dampen a clean cloth with water and a small amount of mild detergent or baby shampoo. Gently dab the stained area, being careful not to rub too vigorously, as this may damage the fibers. Once the stain has lifted, rinse the area with clean water and pat dry with a towel.

Step 2: Hand Washing:

If your hat is made of delicate fibers or has intricate designs, it's best to hand wash it to avoid any potential damage. Fill a basin or sink with lukewarm water and add a small amount of mild detergent or baby shampoo. Submerge your hat in the soapy water and gently agitate it for a few minutes, ensuring that the detergent reaches all areas. Avoid twisting or wringing the hat, as this can cause it to lose its shape. Rinse the hat thoroughly with clean water until all soap residue is removed.

Step 3: Machine Washing (Optional):

If your hat is made of sturdier materials, such as acrylic or cotton, you may choose to machine wash it. However, it's crucial to use a gentle cycle and place your hat in a mesh laundry bag to protect it from getting tangled or stretched.

Guide: Properly Storing Feline Hats to Maintain Their Quality and Condition

Introduction:

Feline hats are not only adorable accessories for our beloved cats, but they also serve a practical purpose by protecting them from the elements. To ensure that these hats remain in good condition and last for a long time, it is essential to store them properly. In this guide, we will provide you with detailed instructions on how to store feline hats to maintain their quality and keep them looking their best.

Step 1: Clean the Hat

Before storing a feline hat, it is crucial to clean it thoroughly. Use a soft brush or cloth to remove any dirt, dust, or pet hair from the hat's surface. If the hat is machine washable, follow the manufacturer's instructions for cleaning. For hats that cannot be washed, spot clean them using a mild detergent and water. Allow the hat to dry completely before proceeding to the next step.

Step 2: Choose the Right Storage Container

Selecting the appropriate storage container is essential to protect the feline hat from damage. Opt for a container that is clean, dry, and free from any odors. A plastic or fabric storage box with a lid is ideal for this purpose. Avoid using cardboard boxes as they can attract pests and may not provide adequate protection against moisture.

Step 3: Line the Container

To provide extra protection for the feline hat, line the storage container with acid-free tissue paper or clean cotton fabric. This will help prevent any potential color transfer or damage to the hat's material. Gently place the hat on top of the lining, ensuring it is centered and not folded or creased.

Step 4: Add Additional Padding

If the feline hat is delicate or has intricate details, consider adding additional padding to protect it from any potential damage. You can use soft, clean socks or bubble wrap to provide cushioning around the hat. Make sure the padding is not too tight or compressing the hat, as this can cause deformation.

Step 5: Store in a Cool, Dry Place

Find a suitable location to store the feline hat, away from direct sunlight, extreme temperatures, and high humidity. Exposure to these elements can cause fading, discoloration, and deterioration of the hat's material. A closet or a shelf in a climate-controlled room would be an ideal choice.

Guide: Repairing and Refreshing Worn Items in Crochet Hat for Your Cat:

Introduction:

Crocheting hats for your cat can be a fun and creative way to keep them warm and stylish. However, over time, these hats may start to show signs of wear and tear. Instead of throwing them away and starting from scratch, why not try repairing and refreshing them? In this guide, we will provide you with step-by-step instructions on how to repair and refresh worn crochet hats for your cat, so they can continue to enjoy their fashionable headwear.

Materials Needed:

1. Worn crochet hat for your cat

2. Crochet hook (appropriate size for the yarn used)

3. Yarn (matching or complementary color)

4. Scissors

5. Yarn needle

Step 1: Assess the Damage

Before you begin repairing the hat, carefully examine it to identify any areas that need attention. Look for loose stitches, holes, or areas where the yarn has unraveled. Take note of these areas, as they will be the focus of your repair work.

Step 2: Gather the Necessary Supplies

Once you have assessed the damage, gather all the materials needed for the repair. Make sure you have the appropriate crochet hook size for the yarn used in the hat, as well as a matching or complementary color of yarn. Having a yarn needle and scissors on hand will also be helpful for weaving in ends and trimming excess yarn.

Step 3: Repair Loose Stitches

If you notice any loose stitches in the hat, use your crochet hook to carefully tighten them. Insert the hook into the stitch, grab the loose yarn, and pull it through the stitch to tighten it. Repeat this process for all loose stitches, ensuring that the tension is consistent throughout the hat.

Step 4: Fix Holes and Unraveled Areas

For holes or areas where the yarn has unraveled, you will need to do some patchwork. Thread your yarn needle with the matching or complementary color of yarn and carefully weave it through the surrounding stitches, creating a new stitch pattern to fill in the hole or cover the unraveled area. Make sure to secure the ends of the yarn by weaving them in and trimming any excess….

HAT SELECTOR

KNITTED HATS

DINOSAUR

BOBBLE HAT

STRAWBERRY

PUMPKIN

SPORTS CAP

SPRING CHICK

PUNK MOHAWK

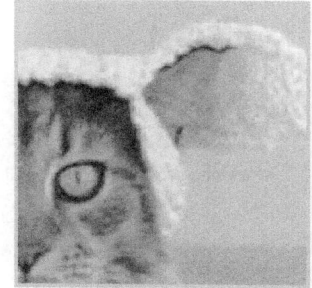
BUNNY

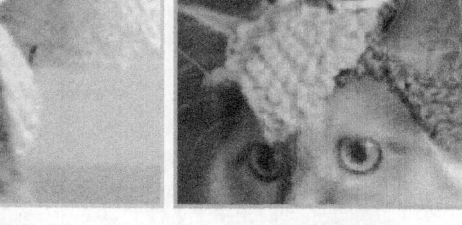
TURKEY

FLOWER CAP

I HEART YOU

EXTRATERRESTRIAL

REINDEER ANTLERS

PARTY HAT

WITCH

METHOD: KNIT

SKILL LEVEL: BEGINNER

Back to Hat Selector

SIZE

TO FIT AN AVERAGE ADULT CAT
- EAR OPENING: 2½ IN. (6 CM)
- WIDTH OF HAT BETWEEN EARS: 2½ IN. (6 CM)

✳✳✳✳✳

SUPPLIES

- 25 YD (23 M) BULKY WEIGHT YARN IN A (GREEN)
- 10 YD (9 M) WORSTED WEIGHT YARN IN B (ORANGE)
- SIZE 7 (4.5 MM) KNITTING NEEDLES
- SIZE 5 (3.75 MM) KNITTING NEEDLES
- SIZE F5 (3.75 MM) CROCHET HOOK
- YARN NEEDLE

FOR THE CAT THAT GOES RAWR! THIS SIMPLE DESIGN IS GREAT FOR HALLOWEEN, OR ANYTIME!

DINOSAUR

BASE
Using yarn A and size 7 (4.5 mm) needles, cast on 3 sts, leaving a 25 in. (64 cm) tail.
Row 1: Knit.
Row 2: Kfb, k to last st, kfb. (5 sts)
Rep last 2 rows five more times. (15 sts)

FIRST EAR HOLE
Row 13: K3, bind off next 10 sts, k last st.
Row 14: K2, cast on 10 sts, k3. (The 3 st side is the front of the hat.)

MIDDLE SECTION
Knit 16 rows.

SECOND EAR HOLE
Row 31: K3, bind off next 10 sts, k last st.
Row 32: K2, cast on 10 sts, k3.
Row 33: Knit.
Row 34: K2tog, k to last 2 sts, k2tog. (13 sts)
Rep last 2 rows five more times. (3 sts)
Bind off, leaving a 25 in. (64 cm) tail.

To create ties, use crochet hook and 25 in. (64 cm) tail, pull a loop through each stitch on bind off edge (3 loops), yo, pull one loop through, work 25ch, pull end through loop tightly, and snip extra yarn. Repeat with other 25 in. (64 cm) tail.

LEEROY MODELS THE DINOSAUR HAT WHILE PLAYING WITH HIS DINOSAUR MODELS.

SPIKES
(Make 3)
Using yarn B and size 5 (3.75 mm) needles, cast on 8 sts.
Rows 1–3: Knit.
Row 4: K2tog, k4, k2tog. (6 sts)
Rows 5–7: Knit.
Row 8: K2tog, k2, k2tog. (4 sts)
Row 9: Knit.
Row 10: [K2tog] twice. (2 sts)
Row 11: K2tog.
Fasten off, leaving a 6 in. (15 cm) tail.

ASSEMBLY
Turn the spikes so that the cast on and bind off tails are at the bottom. You will have three dinosaur shaped spikes. The lower edge with both tails is the edge you sew to the hat base.

Starting at the center front of the base, stitch the lower edge of the first spike into place. Weave in both ends to underside of hat and secure. Repeat with other spikes, following center of hat and stitching into lower edge.

SPIKES: 1½ X 1½ IN. (4 X 4 CM)

METHOD: KNIT

SKILL LEVEL: BEGINNER

Back to Hat Selector

SIZE
TO FIT A SMALL ADULT CAT
- EAR OPENING: 2 IN. (5 CM)
- WIDTH OF HAT BETWEEN EARS: 2 IN. (5 CM)

✹✹✹✹✹

SUPPLIES
- 20 YD (18 M) WORSTED WEIGHT YARN IN A (BLUE)
- 5 YD (4.5 M) WORSTED WEIGHT YARN IN B (RED)
- SIZE 7 (4.5 MM) KNITTING NEEDLES
- YARN NEEDLE
- POM POM MAKER (OPTIONAL)

DOES YOUR CAT GET FRISKY ABOUT COLDER WEATHER? THEN HE MIGHT APPRECIATE THIS CLASSIC

WINTER STYLE, WITH A CATTY TWIST!

BOBBLE HAT

BASE
Using yarn A, cast on 3 sts, leaving a 10 in. (25 cm) tail.
Row 1: Knit.
Row 2: Kfb, k to last st, kfb. (5 sts)
Rep last 2 rows five more times. (15 sts)

FIRST EAR HOLE
Row 13: K3, bind off next 10 sts, k last st.
Row 14: K2, cast on 10 sts, k3. (The 3 st side is the front of the hat.)

MIDDLE SECTION
Knit 16 rows.

SECOND EAR HOLE
Row 31: K3, bind off next 10 sts, k last st.
Row 32: K2, cast on 10 sts, k3.
Row 33: Knit.
Row 34: K2tog, k to last 2 sts, k2tog. (13 sts)
Rep last 2 rows five more times. (3 sts)
Bind off, leaving a 10 in. (25 cm) tail.

POM POM: 1 IN. (2.5 CM) DIAMETER

BRAIDED TRIM: 26 IN. (66 CM) TOTAL LENGTH

LUNA CHECKS THE WEATHER TO SEE IF IT'S WORTH LEAVING HER COZY DEN IN ORDER TO PLAY OUTSIDE.

BRAIDED TRIM
Cut 3 x 36 in. (91 cm) pieces from both yarn A and B (6 strands total). Holding strands together, knot approximately 1 in. (2.5 cm) from top. Holding pairs of strands together, braid a 3-ply braid until trim measures 26 in. (66 cm). Knot, and trim tassel lengths. Stitch to the front edge of base, using cast on and bind off tails to sew into place. Center trim to the center of the hat. You should be left with approximately 7½ in. (19 cm) ties on both sides. Weave tails into the underside of the hat and snip.

Make a 1 in. (2.5 cm) pom pom from yarn A and B, and attach to the center of the base. Now enjoy, take lots of pictures, and give your sweet cat a treat for being such a handsome model!

SOMETHING HAS CAUGHT GUS'S EYE...

METHOD: KNIT

SKILL LEVEL: BEGINNER

Back to Hat Selector

SIZE
TO FIT AN AVERAGE ADULT CAT
- EAR OPENING: 2½ IN. (6 CM)
- WIDTH OF HAT BETWEEN EARS: 2½ IN. (6 CM)

✳✳✳✳✳

SUPPLIES
- 25 YD (23 M) WORSTED WEIGHT YARN IN A (RED)
- 10 YD (9 M) WORSTED WEIGHT YARN IN B (GREEN)
- 3 YD (2.7 M) WORSTED WEIGHT YARN IN C (WHITE)
- SIZE 7 (4.5 MM) KNITTING NEEDLES
- SIZE 5 (3.75 MM) DPNS
- SIZE F5 (3.75 MM) CROCHET HOOK
- YARN NEEDLE

A KITSCHY SUMMER DESIGN! YOU CAN LEAVE THE SEEDS OFF THE DESIGN AND IT WILL DOUBLE AS A TOMATO.

STRAWBERRY

BASE
Using yarn A and size 7 (4.5 mm) needles, cast on 3 sts, leaving a 25 in. (64 cm) tail.
Row 1: Knit.
Row 2: Kfb, k to last st, kfb. (5 sts)
Rep last 2 rows four more times. (13 sts)

FIRST EAR HOLE
Row 11: K2, bind off next 9 sts, k last st.
Row 12: K2, cast on 9 sts, k2.

MIDDLE SECTION
Knit 16 rows.

SECOND EAR HOLE
Row 29: K2, bind off next 9 sts, k last st.
Row 30: K2, cast on 9 sts, k2.
Row 31: Knit.
Row 32: K2tog, k to last 2 sts, k2tog. (11 sts)
Rep last 2 rows four more times. (3 sts)
Bind off, leaving a 25 in. (64 cm) tail.

To create ties, use crochet hook and 25 in. (64 cm) tail, pull a loop through each stitch on bind off edge (3 loops), yo, pull one loop through, work 25ch, pull end through loop tightly, and snip extra yarn. Repeat with other 25 in. (64 cm) tail.

STEM
Using yarn B and two size 5 (3.75 mm) dpns, cast on 4 sts and knit a row. Do not turn needle. Slide the 4 sts to other end of needle, bring yarn around from the back, and knit the 4 sts again. This forms the i-cord technique. Knit in i-cord technique, until stem measures 2 in. (5 cm). You may find it helpful to pull on the cast on edge after every few rows to help the shape. Once complete, snip a 10 in. (25 cm) tail and pull through all 4 loops on the needle. Weave bind off tail through to bottom of stem. You will use this tail to stitch the stem to the base.

LEAVES
(Make 3)
Using yarn B and two size 5 (3.75 mm) dpns, cast on 5 sts.

Rows 1–2: Knit.
Row 3: K2tog, k1, k2tog. (3 sts)
Row 4: Knit.
Row 5: K2tog, k1. (2 sts)
Row 6: K2tog.
Fasten off, leaving a 6 in. (15 cm) tail. Weave through sides of leaf to cast on edge.

ASSEMBLY

Using the bind off tail from the stem, stitch it onto the center of the base. Stitch securely around the cast on edges of the stem. Once complete, pull the cast on and bind off stem tails to the underside of the hat and secure.

Attach leaves to the base of the hat, around the bottom of the stem, by stitching through the cast on edge of the leaves. Use the longer tail to stitch. Weave all ends to the underside of hat and secure.

To finish the hat, thread yarn needle with yarn C. Make short, well-placed stitches on the base of the hat to represent the seeds. Do not do too many—use the photo for reference if necessary. Secure yarn to the underside of the hat.

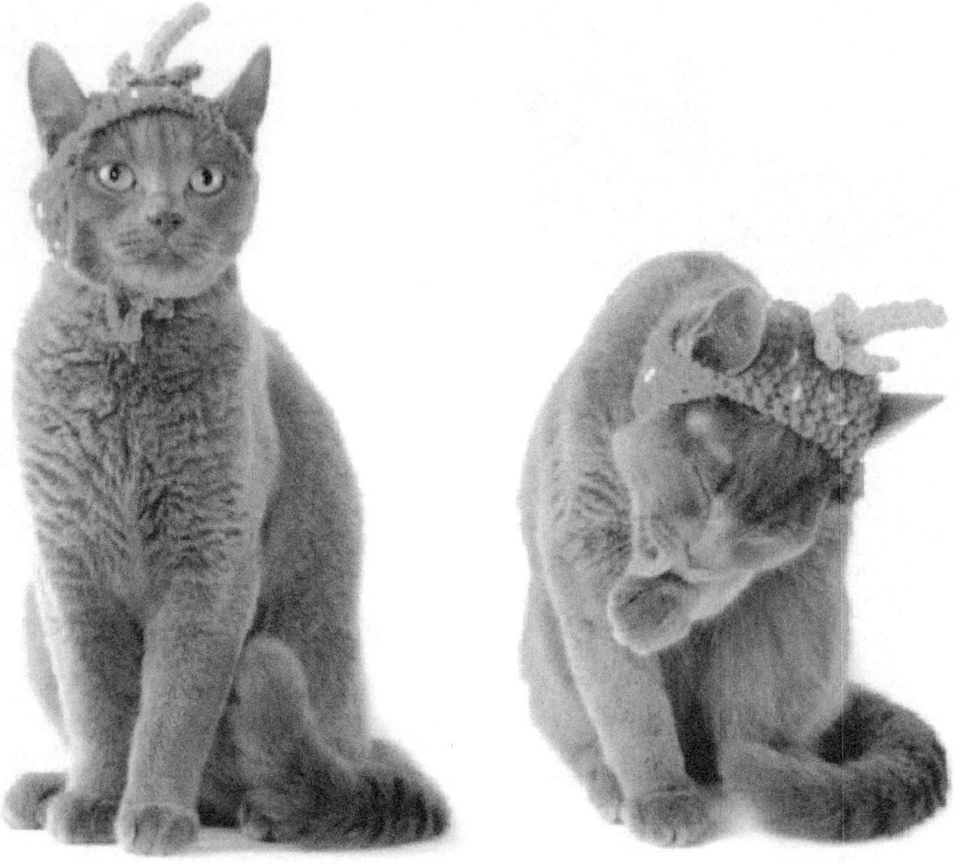

METHOD: KNIT

SKILL LEVEL: BEGINNER

Back to Hat Selector

SIZE

TO FIT AN AVERAGE ADULT CAT
- **EAR OPENING: 2½ IN. (6 CM)**
- **WIDTH OF HAT BETWEEN EARS: 2½ IN. (6 CM)**

✼✼✼✼✼

SUPPLIES

- **25 YD (23 M) WORSTED WEIGHT YARN IN A (ORANGE)**
- **10 YD (9 M) WORSTED WEIGHT YARN IN B (GREEN)**
- **SIZE 7 (4.5 MM) KNITTING NEEDLES**
- **SIZE 5 (3.75 MM) DPNS**
- **SIZE F5 (3.75 MM) CROCHET HOOK**
- **YARN NEEDLE**

FOR YOUR LITTLE PURR PUMPKIN! KNIT THIS IN A VARIETY OF FALL COLORS FOR ALL THE LITTLE PUMPKINS IN YOUR PATCH.

PUMPKIN

BASE
Using yarn A and size 7 (4.5 mm) needles, cast on 3 sts, leaving a 25 in. (64 cm) tail.
Row 1: Knit.
Row 2: Kfb, k to last st, kfb. (5 sts)
Rep last 2 rows four more times. (13 sts)

FIRST EAR HOLE
Row 11: K2, bind off next 9 sts, k last st.
Row 12: K2, cast on 9 sts, k2.

MIDDLE SECTION
Knit 16 rows.

SECOND EAR HOLE
Row 29: K2, bind off next 9 sts, k last st.
Row 30: K2, cast on 9 sts, k2.
Row 31: Knit.
Row 32: K2tog, k to last 2 sts, k2tog. (11 sts)
Rep last 2 rows four more times. (3 sts)
Bind off, leaving a 25 in. (64 cm) tail.
To create ties, use crochet hook and 25 in. (64 cm) tail, pull a loop through each stitch on bind off edge (3 loops), yo, pull one loop through, work 25ch, pull end through loop tightly, and snip extra yarn. Repeat with other 25 in. (64 cm) tail.

STEM
Using yarn B and two size 5 (3.75 mm) dpns, cast on 4 sts and knit a row. Do not turn needle. Slide the 4 sts to other end of needle, bring yarn around from the back, and knit the 4 sts again. This forms the i-cord technique.

STEM: 2 IN.
(5 CM) I-CORD

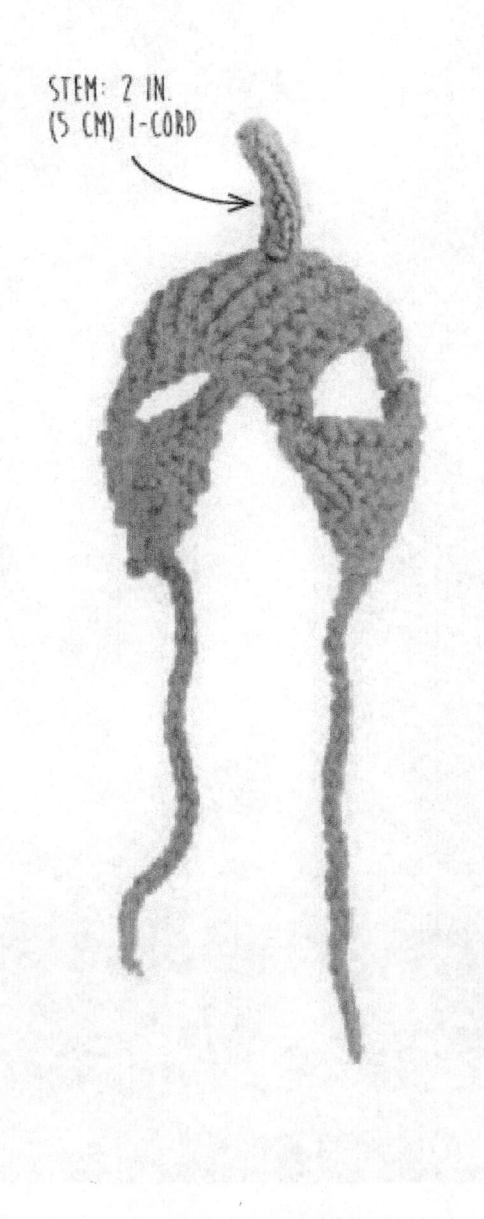

LEEROY BASKS IN THE FALL SUNLIGHT IN THE PUMPKIN HAT.

Knit i-cord, until stem measures 2 in. (5 cm). You may find it helpful to pull on the cast on edge after every few rows to help the shape. Once complete, snip a 10 in. (25 cm) tail and pull through all 4 loops on the needle. Weave bind off tail through to bottom of stem. You will use this tail to stitch the stem to the base.

ASSEMBLY
Using the bind off tail from the stem, stitch it onto the center of the base. Stitch securely around the cast on edges of the stem. Once complete, pull the cast on and bind off stem tails to the underside of the hat and secure.

TENSIONS ARE HIGH AS LUNA WATCHES THE CLOSING MOMENTS OF THE BASEBALL GAME.

METHOD: KNIT

SKILL LEVEL: BEGINNER

Back to Hat Selector

SIZE

TO FIT A SMALL ADULT CAT
- EAR OPENING: 2 IN. (5 CM)
- WIDTH OF HAT BETWEEN EARS: 2 IN. (5 CM)

✾✾✾✾✾

SUPPLIES

- 15 YD (14 M) WORSTED WEIGHT YARN IN A (RED)
- 15 YD (14 M) WORSTED WEIGHT YARN IN B (WHITE)
- 15 YD (14 M) WORSTED WEIGHT YARN IN C (BLUE)
- SIZE 7 (4.5 MM) KNITTING NEEDLES
- SIZE G6 (4 MM) CROCHET HOOK
- YARN NEEDLE

KNIT THIS QUICK PROJECT UP IN YOUR FAVORITE SPORTS TEAM COLORS!

SPORTS CAP

BASE
Using yarn A, cast on 3 sts, leaving a 25 in. (64 cm) tail.
Row 1: Knit.
Row 2: Kfb, k to last st, kfb. (5 sts)
Rep last 2 rows five more times. (15 sts)

FIRST EAR HOLE
Row 13: K2, bind off next 11 sts, k last st.
Row 14: K2, cast on 11 sts, k2.

MIDDLE SECTION
Knit 1 row.
Change to yarn B.
Knit 14 rows.
Change to yarn C.
Knit 1 row.

SECOND EAR HOLE
Row 31: K2, bind off next 11 sts, k last st.
Row 32: K2, cast on 11 sts, k2.
Row 33: Knit.
Row 34: K2tog, k to last 2 sts, k2tog. (13 sts)
Rep last 2 rows five more times. (3 sts)
Bind off, leaving a 25 in. (64 cm) tail.

To create ties, use crochet hook and 25 in. (64 cm) tail, pull a loop through each stitch on bind off edge (3 loops), yo, pull one loop through, work 25ch, pull end through loop tightly, and snip extra yarn. Repeat with other 25 in. (64 cm) tail.

METHOD: KNIT

SKILL LEVEL: INTERMEDIATE

Back to Hat Selector

SIZE

TO FIT AN AVERAGE ADULT CAT
- EAR OPENING: 2½ IN. (6 CM)
- WIDTH OF HAT BETWEEN EARS: 2½ IN. (6 CM)

✶✶✶✶✶

SUPPLIES

- 25 YD (23 M) FAUX FUR YARN IN A (YELLOW)
- 10 YD (9 M) WORSTED WEIGHT YARN IN B (BLACK)
- 10 YD (9 M) WORSTED WEIGHT YARN IN C (ORANGE)
- SIZE 8 (5 MM) KNITTING NEEDLES
- SIZE G6 (4 MM) CROCHET HOOK
- YARN NEEDLE

MAKE SURE TO CHOOSE A TEXTURED YARN FOR THIS PROJECT—IT MAKES ALL THE DIFFERENCE IN ACHIEVING AN ULTRA-FLUFFY CHICK!

GRACIE STRIKES A POSE TO MODEL THE SPRING CHICK HAT.

SPRING CHICK

BASE
Using yarn A, cast on 3 sts, leaving a 25 in. (64 cm) tail.
Row 1: Knit.
Row 2: Kfb, k to last st, kfb. (5 sts)
Rep last 2 rows five more times. (15 sts)
FIRST EAR HOLE
Row 13: K2, bind off next 11 sts, k last st.

Row 14: K2, cast on 11 sts, k2.

MIDDLE SECTION

Knit 16 rows.

SECOND EAR HOLE

Row 31: K2, bind off next 11 sts, k last st.
Row 32: K2, cast on 11 sts, k2.
Row 33: Knit.
Row 34: K2tog, k to last 2 sts, k2tog. (13 sts)
Rep last 2 rows five more times. (3 sts)
Bind off, leaving a 25 in. (64 cm) tail.

To create ties, use crochet hook and 25 in. (64 cm) tail, pull a loop through each stitch on bind off edge (3 loops), yo, pull one loop through, work 25ch, pull end through loop tightly, and snip extra yarn. Repeat with other 25 in. (64 cm) tail.

EYES
(Make 2)
Using yarn B and crochet hook, make a magic ring.
Rnd 1: 1ch, 6sc in ring, sl st in first ch.
Rnd 2: 1ch, [2sc in first st, 1sc] 3 times, sl st in first sc.
Fasten off, leaving a 7 in. (18 cm) tail.

BEAK
Using yarn C, cast on 12 sts, leaving a 10 in. (25 cm) tail.
Rows 1–2: Knit.
Row 3: K2tog, k8, k2tog. (10 sts)
Row 4: Knit.
Row 5: K2tog, k6, k2tog. (8 sts)
Row 6: Knit.
Row 7: K2tog, k4, k2tog. (6 sts)
Rows 8–9: Knit.
Row 10: K2tog, k2, k2tog. (4 sts)
Row 11: Knit.
Row 12: [K2tog] twice. (2 sts)
Bind off, leaving a 6 in. (15 cm) tail.

ASSEMBLY

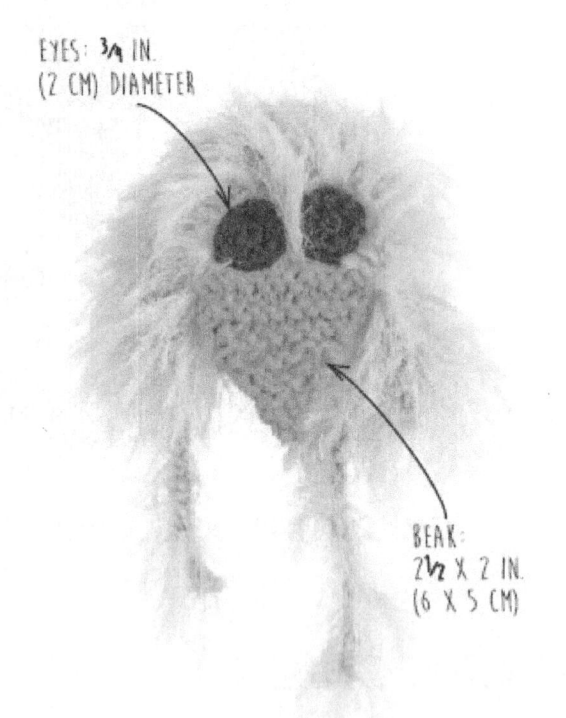

EYES: 3/4 IN. (2 CM) DIAMETER

BEAK: 2½ X 2 IN. (6 X 5 CM)

BEAK

Lay the beak so that both the cast on and bind off tail are upright. This is the top of the beak. Place beak, top side up, along the front of the base, in the middle, about ½ in. (1 cm) from edge (either side can be the front of the hat). Using the 10 in. (25 cm) tail and a yarn needle, stitch along the edges of the beak that are laying on the hat. Also use the 6 in. (15 cm) tail. Attach securely.

EYES

Place eyes so that they are just above the top of the beak, evenly spaced. Attach securely with yarn tails and yarn needle.

METHOD: KNIT

SKILL LEVEL: INTERMEDIATE

Back to Hat Selector

SIZE

TO FIT AN AVERAGE ADULT CAT
- **EAR OPENING: 2½ IN. (6 CM)**
- **WIDTH OF HAT BETWEEN EARS: 2½ IN. (6 CM)**

✵✵✵✵✵

SUPPLIES
- **25 YD (23 M) WORSTED WEIGHT YARN IN A (BLACK)**
- **15 YD (14 M) BULKY WEIGHT YARN IN B (PINK)**
- **SIZE 7 (4.5 MM) KNITTING NEEDLES**
- **SIZE G6 (4 MM) CROCHET HOOK**
- **YARN NEEDLE**

FOR THE ULTIMATE ANARCHIST IN YOUR FAMILY, KNIT UP A PUNK ROCKER FAUX HAWK IN SHOCKING PINK!

PUNK MOHAWK

BASE
Using yarn A, cast on 3 sts, leaving a 25 in. (64 cm) tail.
Row 1: Knit.
Row 2: Kfb, k to last st, kfb. (5 sts)
Rep last 2 rows five more times. (15 sts)
FIRST EAR HOLE
Row 13: K3, bind off next 10 sts, k last st.
Row 14: K2, cast on 10 sts, k3. (The 3 st side is the front of the hat.)
MIDDLE SECTION
Knit 16 rows.
SECOND EAR HOLE
Row 31: K3, bind off next 10 sts, k last st.
Row 32: K2, cast on 10 sts, k3.
Row 33: Knit.
Row 34: K2tog, k to last 2 sts, k2tog. (13 sts)
Rep last 2 rows five more times. (3 sts)
Bind off, leaving a 25 in. (64 cm) tail.

Using crochet hook, work 25ch on each side using the 25 in. (64 cm) tails left at the beginning and end of your work. This creates the ties for your cat hat.

FAUX HAWK
Using yarn B, clip fifteen to twenty 2 in. (5 cm) pieces. You will attach these pieces to the center garter stitch ridge of your cat hat base.

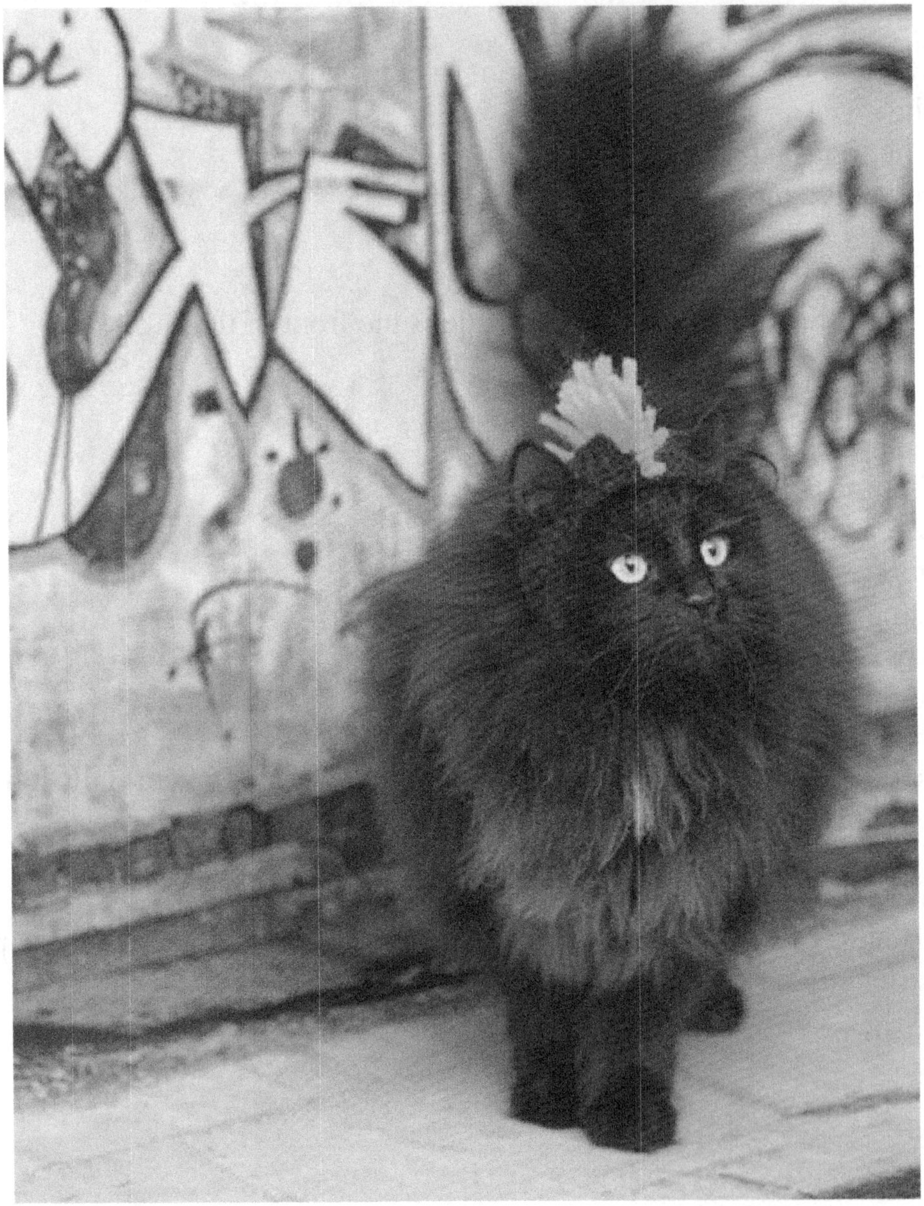

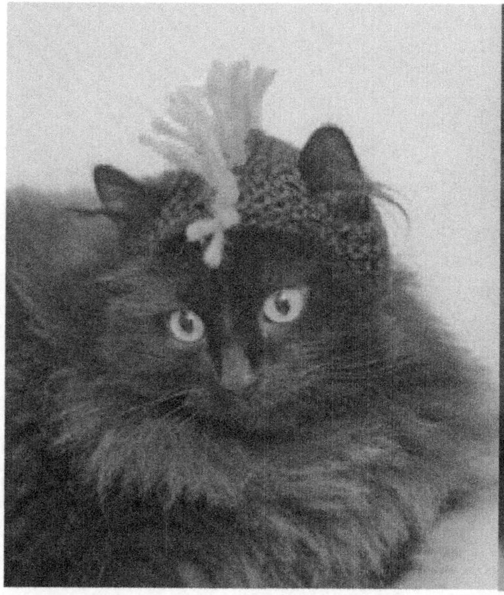
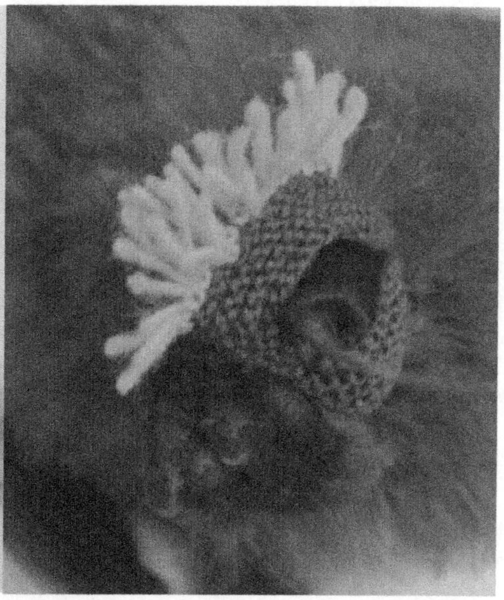

ASSEMBLY

You will attach the faux hawk pieces in a manner similar to attaching fringe to a scarf. To attach, slide crochet hook underneath the first stitch in the center garter stitch ridge on the base of the hat. Take a 2 in. (5 cm) piece of yarn, fold it in half, and pull the loop through the garter row using the crochet hook. Take the ends of the faux hawk yarn and pull them through the loop so that it is securely knotted. The faux hawk yarn should stand upright using this method. Repeat, cutting more 2 in. (5 cm) pieces if necessary, and continue attaching them down the center garter stitch row.

To create a fuller faux hawk, clip more yarn and attach it to both sides of the center garter stitch ridge. When finished, trim faux hawk to a uniform length (about 1 in./2.5 cm).

FAUX HAWK PIECES:
2 IN. (5 CM) LONG

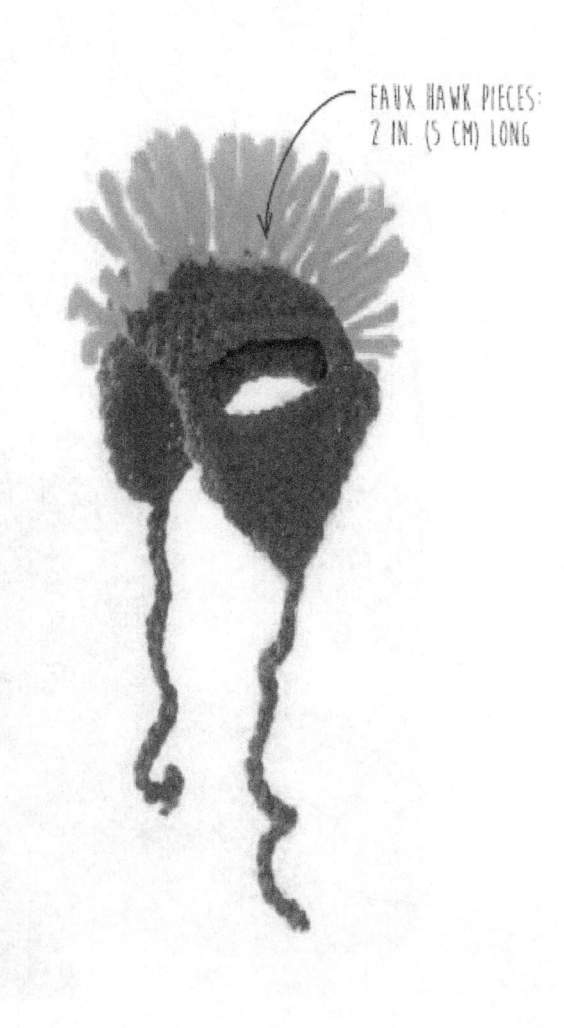

JASPER PACES THE SIDEWALK WITH PRIDE IN HIS PUNK MOHAWK HAT.

METHOD: KNIT

SKILL LEVEL: INTERMEDIATE

Back to Hat Selector

SIZE
TO FIT AN AVERAGE ADULT CAT
- EAR OPENING: 2½ IN. (6 CM)
- WIDTH OF HAT BETWEEN EARS: 2½ IN. (6 CM)

✳✳✳✳✳

SUPPLIES
- 40 YD (37 M) MEDIUM WEIGHT YARN IN CREAM
- SIZE 7 (4.5 MM) KNITTING NEEDLES
- SIZE G6 (4 MM) CROCHET HOOK
- YARN NEEDLE

IF YOUR EARS HANG LOW, THIS BUNNY HAT WILL BE THE PERFECT FIT!

BUNNY

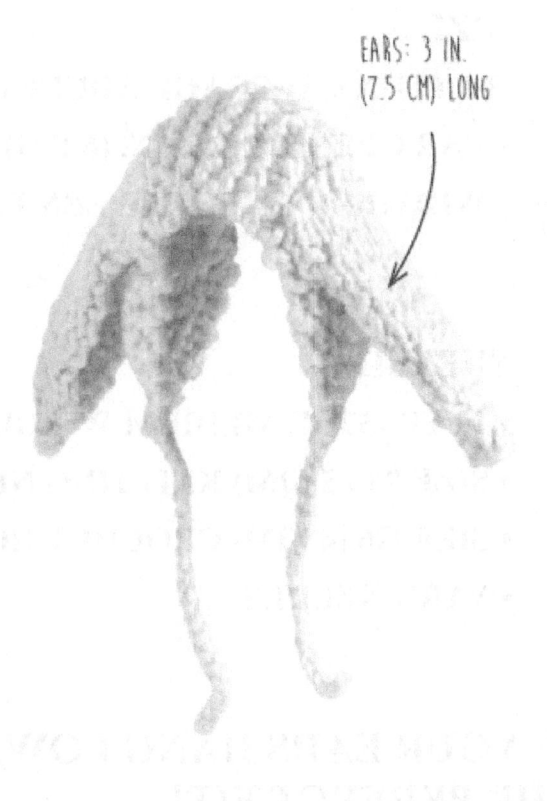

BASE
Cast on 3 sts, leaving a 25 in. (64 cm) tail.
Row 1: Knit.
Row 2: Kfb, k to last st, kfb. (5 sts)
Rep last 2 rows five more times. (15 sts)
FIRST EAR HOLE
Row 13: K2, bind off next 11 sts, k last st.
Row 14: K2, cast on 11 sts, k2.
MIDDLE SECTION
Knit 16 rows.
SECOND EAR HOLE
Row 31: K2, bind off next 11 sts, k last st.
Row 32: K2, cast on 11 sts, k2.
Row 33: Knit.
Row 34: K2tog, k to last 2 sts, k2tog. (13 sts)
Rep last 2 rows five more times. (3 sts)
Bind off, leaving a 25 in. (64 cm) tail.

To create ties, use crochet hook and 25 in. (64 cm) tail, pull a loop through each stitch on bind off edge (3 loops), yo, pull one loop through, work 25ch, pull end through loop tightly, and snip extra yarn. Repeat with other 25 in. (64 cm) tail.

EARS
(Make 2)
Cast on 13 sts, leaving a 10 in. (25 cm) tail (you will use this tail to attach the ear to the base of the hat later).
Row 1: Knit.
Row 2: Purl.
Rep last 2 rows once more.
Row 5: K1, k2tog, k7, k2tog, k1. (11 sts)
Row 6: Purl.
Row 7: Knit.
Row 8: Purl.
Rep last 2 rows three more times.
Row 15: K1, k2tog, k5, k2tog, k1. (9 sts)
Row 16: Purl.
Row 17: Knit.
Row 18: Purl.

EARS: 3 IN.
(7.5 CM) LONG

Row 19: K1, k2tog, k3, k2tog, k1. (7 sts)
Row 20: Purl.
Row 21: K1, k2tog, k1, k2tog, k1. (5 sts)
Row 22: Purl.
Bind off, leaving a 6 in. (15 cm) tail.

Using yarn needle, weave in bind off tail.
Adjust the ear length in this pattern by increasing (or decreasing) between Rows 7 and 14.

ASSEMBLY
To attach ears, use cast on tail and yarn needle to stitch one ear to the middle section of the base, centered above ear opening and with knit side uppermost. Secure both ends around ear opening (so that ear is slightly curved down). Stitch the ear along the cast on edge, placing it on the first garter row above the ear opening. Repeat with second ear and other ear opening.

WHO IS THIS HANDSOME FURBALL? IT'S HUCK MODELING THE BUNNY HAT.

METHOD: KNIT

SKILL LEVEL: INTERMEDIATE

Back to Hat Selector

SIZE

TO FIT AN AVERAGE ADULT CAT
- EAR OPENING: 2½ IN. (6 CM)
- WIDTH OF HAT BETWEEN EARS: 2½ IN. (6 CM)

✳✳✳✳✳

SUPPLIES

- 25 YD (23 M) BULKY WEIGHT YARN IN A (BROWN)
- 10 YD (9 M) WORSTED WEIGHT YARN IN B (RED)
- 10 YD (9 M) WORSTED WEIGHT YARN IN C (BLACK)
- 15 YD (14 M) WORSTED WEIGHT YARN IN D (ORANGE)
- 10 YD (9 M) WORSTED WEIGHT YARN IN E (WHITE)
- SIZE 7 (4.5 MM) KNITTING NEEDLES
- SIZE G6 (4 MM) CROCHET HOOK
- YARN NEEDLE

THE CUTEST LITTLE TURKEY YOU EVER DID SEE! A REAL CENTERPIECE FOR ANY THANKSGIVING CELEBRATION!

TURKEY

BASE
Using yarn A, cast on 3 sts, leaving a 6 in. (15 cm) tail.
Row 1: Knit.
Row 2: Kfb, k to last st, kfb. (5 sts)
Rep last 2 rows five more times. (15 sts)
FIRST EAR HOLE
Row 13: K2, bind off next 11 sts, k last st.
Row 14: K2, cast on 11 sts, k2.
MIDDLE SECTION
Knit 16 rows.
SECOND EAR HOLE
Row 31: K2, bind off next 11 sts, k last st.
Row 32: K2, cast on 11 sts, k2.
Row 33: Knit.
Row 34: K2tog, k to last 2 sts, k2tog. (13 sts)
Rep last 2 rows five more times. (3 sts)
Bind off, leaving a 6 in. (15 cm) tail.

To create ties, cut two pieces of yarn B measuring 30 in. (76 cm) each. With crochet hook and one piece of yarn, pull a loop through the end of the base and work 25ch. Pull yarn through last loop tightly and trim. Weave in starting end to underside of the hat. Repeat on other side.

OUTER EYES
(Make 2)
Using yarn E and crochet hook, make a magic ring.
Rnd 1: 1ch, 12sc in ring, sl st in first ch.
Rnd 2: 1ch, [2sc in first st, 1sc] 6 times, sl st in first sc.
Cut yarn, leaving a 10 in. (25 cm) tail, and pull tightly through loop.

LYRIC PLAYFULLY MODELS THE TURKEY HAT.

INNER EYES
(Make 2)
Using yarn C and crochet hook, make a magic ring.

Rnd 1: 1ch, 6sc in ring, sl st in first ch.
Rnd 2: 1ch, [2sc in first st, 1sc] 3 times, sl st in first sc.
Cut yarn, leaving a 7 in. (18 cm) tail, and pull tightly through loop.

BEAK
Using yarn D, cast on 12 sts, leaving a 10 in. (25 cm) tail.
Rows 1–2: Knit.
Row 3: K2tog, k8, k2tog. (10 sts)
Row 4: Knit.
Row 5: K2tog, k6, k2tog. (8 sts)
Row 6: Knit.
Row 7: K2tog, k4, k2tog. (6 sts)
Rows 8–9: Knit.
Row 10: K2tog, k2, k2tog. (4 sts)
Row 11: Knit.
Row 12: [K2tog] twice. (2 sts)
Bind off, leaving a 6 in. (15 cm) tail.

ASSEMBLY
BEAK
Lay the beak so that both the cast on and bind off tails are upright. This is the top of the beak. Place beak, top side up, along the front of the base, in the middle, about ½ in (1 cm) from edge (either side can be the front of the hat). Using the 10 in. (25 cm) tail and a yarn needle, stitch along the edges of the beak that are laying on the hat. Also use the 6 in. (15 cm) tail. Attach securely.

EYES

Place eyes so that they are touching the top of the beak, evenly spaced. Attach securely with yarn tails and yarn needle.

GOBBLE

Using yarn B and crochet hook, pull a loop through base at the center of the stitched on edge of the beak. Work 7ch through the beak and base using photo as guide, 3ch, and cut yarn. Weave end through ch sts and to underside of hat.

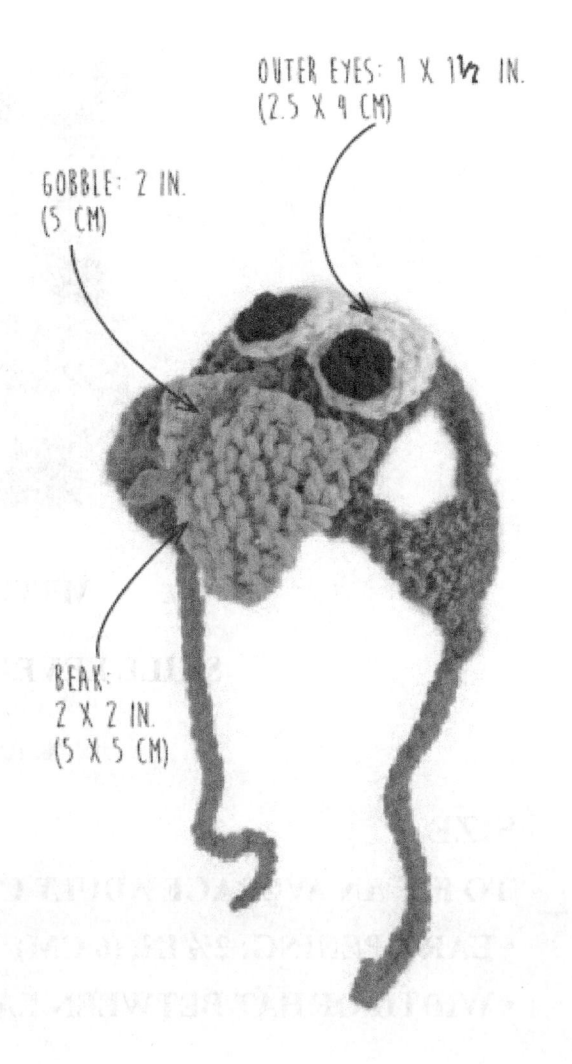

OUTER EYES: 1 X 1½ IN. (2.5 X 4 CM)

GOBBLE: 2 IN. (5 CM)

BEAK: 2 X 2 IN. (5 X 5 CM)

METHOD: KNIT

SKILL LEVEL: INTERMEDIATE

Back to Hat Selector

SIZE

TO FIT AN AVERAGE ADULT CAT

- EAR OPENING: 2½ IN. (6 CM)
- WIDTH OF HAT BETWEEN EARS: 2 IN. (5 CM)

✳✳✳✳✳

SUPPLIES

- 40 YD (37 M) WORSTED WEIGHT YARN IN A (RED)
- 10 YD (9 M) WORSTED WEIGHT YARN IN B (BLUE)
- SIZE 7 (4.5 MM) KNITTING NEEDLES
- SIZE 5 (3.75 MM) KNITTING NEEDLES
- SIZE G6 (4 MM) CROCHET HOOK
- YARN NEEDLE

FOR ALL THOSE COOL CATS OUT THERE IN STYLISH HATS: PUT A FLOWER IN YOUR CAP FOR A SPECIAL FELINE FLOURISH!

FLOWER CAP

BASE
Using yarn A and size 7 (4.5 mm) needles, cast on 3 sts, leaving a 6 in. (15 cm) tail.
Row 1: Knit.
Row 2: Kfb, k to last st, kfb. (5 sts)
Rep last 2 rows five more times. (15 sts)
FIRST EAR HOLE
Row 13: K2, bind off next 11 sts, k last st.
Row 14: K2, cast on 11 sts, k2.
MIDDLE SECTION
Knit 16 rows.
SECOND EAR HOLE
Row 31: K2, bind off next 11 sts, k last st.
Row 32: K2, cast on 11 sts, k2.
Row 33: Knit.
Row 34: K2tog, k to last 2 sts, k2tog. (13 sts)
Rep last 2 rows five more times. (3 sts)
Bind off, leaving a 6 in. (15 cm) tail.

To create ties, cut two pieces of yarn A measuring 30 in. (76 cm) each. With crochet hook and one piece of yarn, pull a loop through the end of the base and work 25ch. Pull yarn through last loop tightly and trim. Weave in starting end to underside of the hat. Repeat on other side.

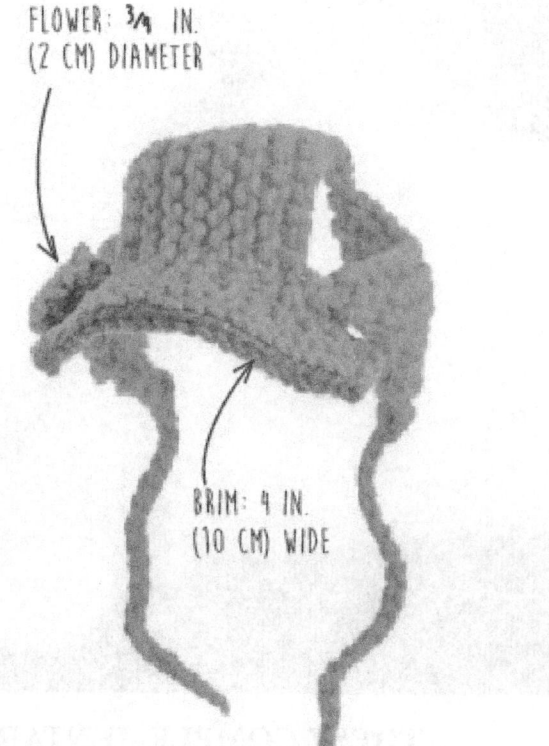

FLOWER: ¾ IN. (2 CM) DIAMETER

BRIM: 4 IN. (10 CM) WIDE

THESE COMPLEMENTARY FLOWER CAPS ARE MODELED BY LYRIC AND LINK.

BRIM

Using yarn A and size 5 (3.75 mm) needles, pick up 12 sts along front of base, starting in front of one ear hole and picking them up evenly until you work your way past the second ear hole.
Knit 1 row.
Row 2: Kfb of each st. (24 sts)
Rows 3–5: Knit.
Row 6: Kfb, k to last st, kfb. (26 sts)
Bind off using yarn B.
Thread ends down the sides of the brim and secure to the underside of the base.

VARIATION

Use yarn B to knit base, yarn A for brim, and bind off brim with yarn B.

FLOWER
Using yarn B and crochet hook, make a magic ring.
Rnd 1: 1ch, 6sc in ring, sl st in first ch.
Rnd 2: [2sc in first st, 1sc] 3 times. Change to yarn A.
Rnd 3: Sc in each st, sl st in first sc.
Cut yarn and pull through loop. Weave in end to center. Attach to the right of the brim.

METHOD: KNIT

SKILL LEVEL: INTERMEDIATE

Back to Hat Selector

SIZE
TO FIT AN AVERAGE ADULT CAT
- **EAR OPENING: 2½ IN. (6 CM)**
- **WIDTH OF HAT BETWEEN EARS: 2½ IN. (6 CM)**

✳✳✳✳✳

SUPPLIES
- **25 YD (23 M) WORSTED WEIGHT YARN IN A (BROWN)**
- **5 YD (4.5 M) WORSTED WEIGHT YARN IN B (RED)**
- **SIZE 7 (4.5 MM) DPNS**
- **SIZE G6 (4 MM) CROCHET HOOK**
- **1 X 6 IN. (15 CM) PIECE OF PIPE CLEANER (PREFERABLY IN A CORRESPONDING COLOR TO YOUR YARN)**
- **YARN NEEDLE**

SHOW YOUR CAT SOME LOVE WITH THIS ADORABLE HEART HAT.

I HEART YOU

BASE
Using yarn A and two dpns, cast on 3 sts, leaving a 25 in. (64 cm) tail.
Row 1: Knit.
Row 2: Kfb, k to last st, kfb. (5 sts)
Rep last 2 rows five more times. (15 sts)

FIRST EAR HOLE
Row 13: K3, bind off next 10 sts, k last st.
Row 14: K2, cast on 10 sts, k3. (The 3 st side is the front of the hat.)

MIDDLE SECTION
Knit 16 rows.

SECOND EAR HOLE
Row 31: K3, bind off next 10 sts, k last st.
Row 32: K2, cast on 10 sts, k3.
Row 33: Knit.
Row 34: K2tog, k to last 2 sts, k2tog. (13 sts)
Rep last 2 rows five more times. (3 sts)
Bind off, leaving a 25 in. (64 cm) tail.

Using crochet hook, work 25ch on each side using the 25 in. (64 cm) tails left at the beginning and end of your work. This creates the ties for your cat hat.

HEART
Using yarn B and two dpns, cast on 4 sts, leaving a 6 in. (15 cm) tail. Knit a row. Do not turn needle. Holding piece of pipe cleaner in place, slide the 4 sts to other end of needle, bring yarn around from the back, encasing the pipe cleaner, and knit the 4 sts again. This forms the i-cord technique. Using the i-cord method, knit around pipe cleaner until only ¼ in. (0.5 cm) of pipe cleaner remains exposed on both ends. Cut yarn, leaving a 6 in. (15 cm) tail, and use yarn needle to pull tail through sts on needle. Bend the i-cord into a heart shape.

HEART: 6 IN. (15 CM) PIPE CLEANER COVERED IN I-CORD

WHO CAN RESIST THE LOVING LOOK OF PERCY?

ASSEMBLY
Using a knitting needle as a guide, poke both ends of the heart through the center of the hat base. Bring the exposed ends back up through the base and twist them around themselves securely. Using a yarn needle, stitch the base of the heart to the base of the hat. Stitch so that the pipe cleaner is no longer exposed and the heart sits upright. Pull both tails through to underside of hat, and knot the ends to anchor the heart.

METHOD: KNIT

SKILL LEVEL: INTERMEDIATE

Back to Hat Selector

SIZE
TO FIT AN AVERAGE ADULT CAT
- EAR OPENING: 2½ IN. (6 CM)
- WIDTH OF HAT BETWEEN EARS: 2½ IN. (6 CM)

✳✳✳✳✳

SUPPLIES
- 35 YD (32 M) WORSTED WEIGHT YARN IN A (GREEN)
- SCRAP OF WORSTED WEIGHT YARN IN B (BLACK)
- SIZE 7 (4.5 MM) KNITTING NEEDLES
- SIZE 3 (3.25 MM) DPNS
- SIZE G6 (4 MM) CROCHET HOOK
- 1 X 3 IN. (7.5 CM) PIECE OF PIPE CLEANER (PREFERABLY IN A CORRESPONDING COLOR TO YOUR YARN)
- YARN NEEDLE
- POLYESTER FIBERFILL

IT'S AN ENCOUNTER OF THE THIRD KIND! KNITTING AROUND A FLEXIBLE PIPE CLEANER ALLOWS YOUR CAT'S THIRD EYE TO PEER IN WHATEVER DIRECTION YOU CHOOSE.

EXTRATERRESTRIAL

BASE
Using yarn A and size 7 (4.5 mm) needles, cast on 3 sts, leaving a 25 in. (64 cm) tail.
Row 1: Knit.
Row 2: Kfb, k to last st, kfb. (5 sts)
Rep last 2 rows five more times. (15 sts)

FIRST EAR HOLE
Row 13: K2, bind off next 11 sts, k last st.
Row 14: K2, cast on 11 sts, k2.

MIDDLE SECTION
Knit 16 rows.

SECOND EAR HOLE
Row 31: K2, bind off next 11 sts, k last st.
Row 32: K2, cast on 11 sts, k2.
Row 33: Knit.
Row 34: K2tog, k to last 2 sts, k2tog. (13 sts)
Rep last 2 rows five more times. (3 sts)
Bind off, leaving a 25 in. (64 cm) tail.

To create ties, use crochet hook and 25 in. (64 cm) tail, pull a loop through each stitch on bind off edge (3 loops), yo, pull one loop through, work 25ch, pull end through loop tightly, and snip extra yarn. Repeat with other 25 in. (64 cm) tail.

EYE
Using yarn A and two size 3 (3.25 mm) dpns, cast on 4 sts, leaving a 15 in. (38 cm) tail. Knit a row. Do not turn needle. Holding piece of pipe cleaner in place, slide the 4 sts to other end of needle, bring yarn around from the back, encasing the pipe cleaner, and knit the 4 sts again. This forms the i-cord technique. Using the i-cord method, knit around pipe cleaner until it is enclosed, leaving ½ in. (1 cm) exposed at the bottom.

EYE: 3 IN. (7.5 CM) PIPE CLEANER, COVERED IN I-CORD

Next row: Kfb of each st. (8 sts) Divide sts onto three dpns and join to work in the round.
Next rnd: Kfb of each st. (16 sts) Knit 3 rnds.
Next rnd: K2tog around. (8 sts) Lightly stuff with polyester fiberfill.
Next rnd: K2tog around. (4 sts) Cut yarn and pull through remaining loops. Weave in end.

Using yarn B and yarn needle, run several long stitches on center of eye ball to create a pupil. Weave in ends.

ASSEMBLY

Center the eye on the base. Poke the exposed pipe cleaner through the base, using a knitting needle as a guide. Bring the exposed end back up through the base and twist it around itself securely. Using a yarn needle and the cast on tail of the i-cord, stitch the eye to the base along the cast on edge of the i-cord. Pull both tails through to underside of the hat, and knot the ends to anchor the eye.

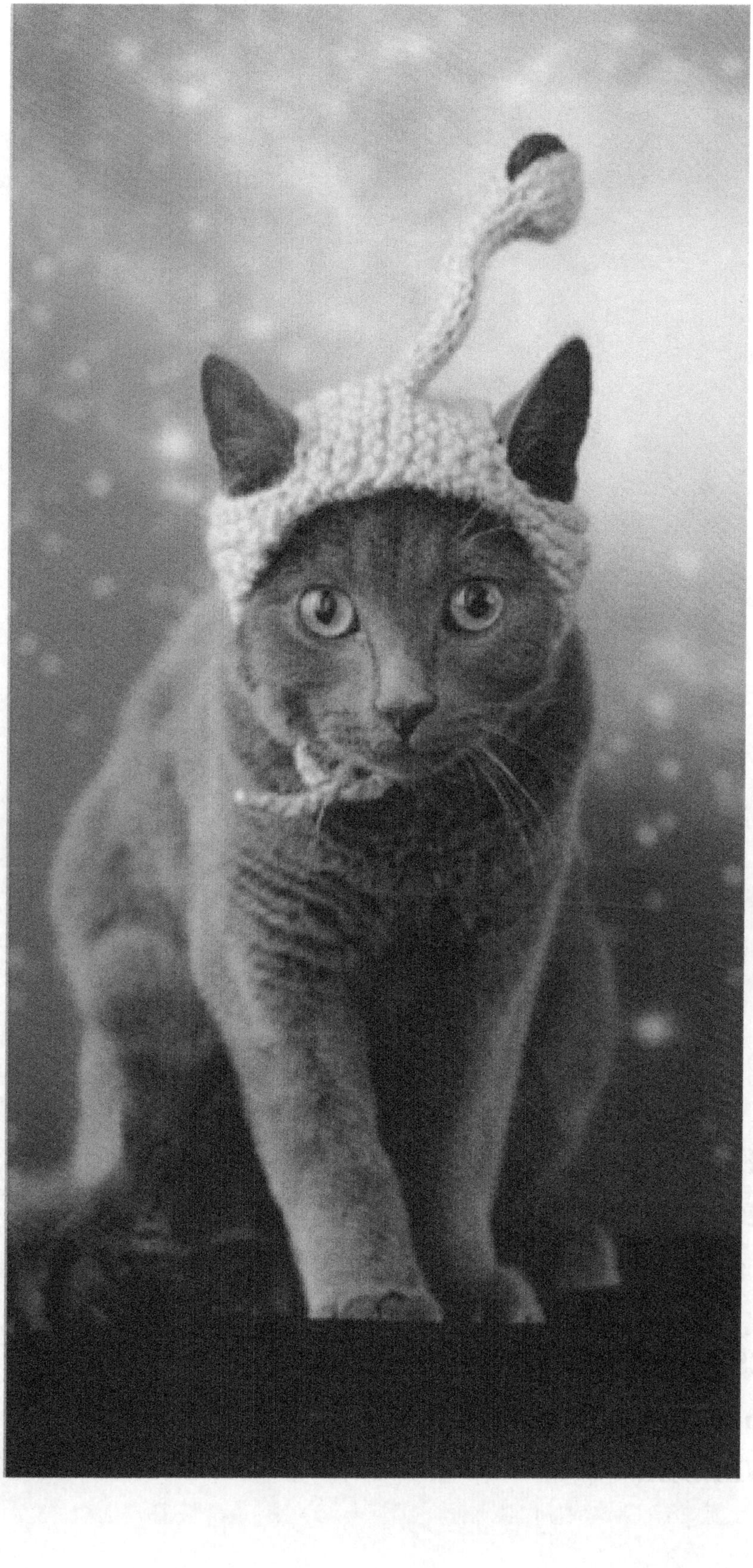

METHOD: KNIT

SKILL LEVEL: INTERMEDIATE

Back to Hat Selector

SIZE
TO FIT A SMALL ADULT CAT
- EAR OPENING: 2 IN. (5 CM)
- WIDTH OF HAT BETWEEN EARS: 2 IN. (5 CM)

✳✳✳✳✳

SUPPLIES
- 30 YD (27 M) WORSTED WEIGHT YARN
- SIZE 7 (4.5 MM) DPNS
- 2 X 4 IN. (10 CM) PIECES OF PIPE CLEANER (PREFERABLY IN A CORRESPONDING COLOR TO YOUR YARN)
- SIZE G6 (4 MM) CROCHET HOOK
- YARN NEEDLE

ANTLERS ARE THE PERFECT HOLIDAY GIFT, GUARANTEED TO INSPIRE SOME HOLIDAY CHEER IN YOUR FAVORITE FELINE!

REINDEER ANTLERS

JASPER HELPS WITH THE WRAPPING IN HIS FESTIVE OUTFIT.

BASE
Using two dpns, cast on 3 sts, leaving a 25 in. (64 cm) tail.

Row 1: Knit.
Row 2: Kfb, k to last st, kfb. (5 sts)
Rep last 2 rows five more times. (15 sts)

FIRST EAR HOLE
Row 13: K3, bind off next 10 sts, k last st.
Row 14: K2, cast on 10 sts, k3. (The 3st side is the front of the hat.)

MIDDLE SECTION
Knit 16 rows.

SECOND EAR HOLE
Row 31: K3, bind off next 10 sts, k last st.
Row 32: K2, cast on 10 sts, k3.
Row 33: Knit.
Row 34: K2tog, k to last 2 sts, k2tog. (13 sts)
Rep last 2 rows five more times. (3 sts)
Bind off, leaving a 25 in. (64 cm) tail.

Using crochet hook, work 25ch on each side using the 25 in. (64 cm) tails left at the beginning and end of your work. This creates the ties for your cat hat.

ANTLERS
(Make 2)
Using two dpns, cast on 4 sts, leaving a 6 in. (15 cm) tail. Knit a row. Do not turn needle. Holding one piece of pipe cleaner in place, slide the 4 sts to other end of needle, bring yarn around from the back, encasing the pipe cleaner, and knit the 4 sts again. This forms the i-cord technique. This technique, when worked with the pipe cleaner in the center, will cover the pipe cleaner and form a bendable antler. Work in this method until pipe cleaner is covered, leaving a ½ in. (1 cm) of pipe cleaner exposed at the bottom for securing antler to the base. To finish, cut 8 in. (20 cm) tail and pull through sts on needle using a yarn needle.
Weave tail through antler, leaving it at the base to stitch antler in place.
Next, pick up 2 sts ¼ in. (0.5 cm) from top of antler and knit 5 rows with i-cord technique.

Weave ends in, pulling through antler to base and clipping so that the ends are not exposed.

ASSEMBLY
With smaller points facing inward, attach antlers as follows. Position antler ¼ in. (0.5 cm) from the ear opening and center the antler on the hat. Poke the exposed pipe cleaner through the base, using a knitting needle as a guide. Bring the exposed end back up through the base and twist it around itself securely. Using a yarn needle, stitch the base of the antler to the base of the hat. Stitch so that the pipe cleaner is no longer exposed

and the antler sits upright. Pull both tails through to underside of hat, and knot the ends to anchor the antler.
Repeat with second antler.

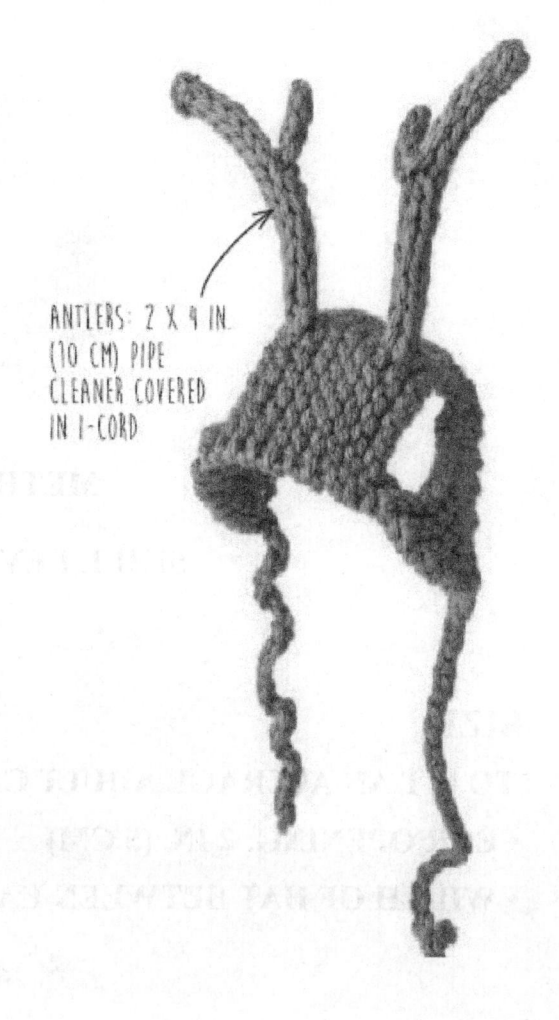

ANTLERS: 2 X 4 IN. (10 CM) PIPE CLEANER COVERED IN I-CORD

METHOD: KNIT

SKILL LEVEL: DIFFICULT

Back to Hat Selector

SIZE

TO FIT AN AVERAGE ADULT CAT

- EAR OPENING: 2 IN. (5 CM)
- WIDTH OF HAT BETWEEN EARS: 2 IN. (5 CM)

✻✻✻✻✻

SUPPLIES

- 25 YD (23 M) WORSTED WEIGHT YARN IN A (PINK)
- 10 YD (9 M) WORSTED WEIGHT YARN IN B (WHITE)
- 10 YD (9 M) WORSTED WEIGHT YARN IN C (MINT)
- SIZE 7 (4.5 MM) DPNS
- SIZE F5 (3.75 MM) CROCHET HOOK
- YARN NEEDLE
- POLYESTER FIBERFILL
- POM POM MAKER (OPTIONAL)

THIS STRIPED HAT IS PURRFECT FOR CAT CELEBRATIONS!

PARTY HAT

BASE
Using yarn A and two dpns, cast on 3 sts, leaving a 25 in. (64 cm) tail.
Row 1: Knit.
Row 2: Kfb, k to last st, kfb. (5 sts)
Rep last 2 rows five more times. (15 sts)

FIRST EAR HOLE
Row 13: K3, bind off next 10 sts, k last st.
Row 14: K2, cast on 10 sts, k3. (The 3 st side is the front of the hat.)

MIDDLE SECTION
Knit 16 rows.

SECOND EAR HOLE
Row 31: K3, bind off next 10 sts, k last st.
Row 32: K2, cast on 10 sts, k3.
Row 33: Knit.
Row 34: K2tog, k to last 2 sts, k2tog. (13 sts)
Rep last 2 rows five more times. (3 sts)
Bind off, leaving a 25 in. (64 cm) tail.

To create ties, use crochet hook and 25 in. (64 cm) tail, pull a loop through each stitch on bind off edge (3 loops), yo, pull one loop through, work 25ch, pull end through loop tightly and snip extra yarn. Repeat with other 25 in. (64 cm) tail.

HAT
Using yarn B, cast on 30 sts leaving a 20 in. (50 cm) tail. Divide onto three dpns (10 sts per needle) and join to work in the round.
Rnds 1–2: Knit.
Rnd 3: [K2tog, k6, k2tog] 3 times. (24 sts)
Rnds 4–7: Knit.
Rnd 8: [K2tog, k4, k2tog] 3 times. (18 sts)
Rnds 9–10: Knit.
Change to yarn A.

Rnds 11–14: Knit.
Rnd 15: [K2, k2tog, k2] 3 times. (15 sts)
Rnds 16–19: Knit.
Rnd 20: [K1, k2tog, k2] 3 times. (12 sts)

Change to yarn C.
Rnds 21–24: Knit.
Rnd 25: [K1, k2tog, k1] 3 times. (9 sts)
Rnds 26–28: Knit.
Rnd 29: [K2tog] 4 times, k1. (5 sts)
Rnd 30: [K2tog] twice, k1. (3 sts)
Cut yarn and pull through sts on needle. Pull closed, and weave end into inside of hat.

ASSEMBLY
Make a 1 in. (2.5 cm) pom pom using all three yarn colors. Secure to top of hat. Weave ends into the inside of the hat and secure in place. Lightly stuff hat with polyester fiberfill. Do not overfill. Using the cast on tail from the hat, stitch the hat onto the middle section of the base. Stitch into the cast on edge of the hat, until hat is securely in place. Weave end through to underside of base and tie securely.

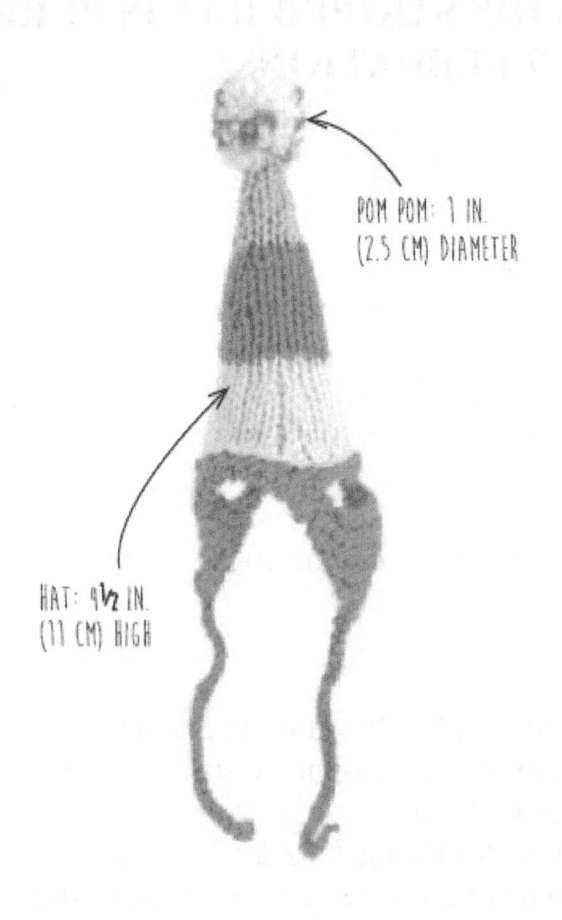

**MOOCH GETS IN THE PARTY MOOD WITH THIS STRIPED
POM POM HAT.**

METHOD: KNIT

SKILL LEVEL: DIFFICULT

Back to Hat Selector

SIZE
TO FIT AN AVERAGE ADULT CAT
- EAR OPENING: 2½ IN. (6 CM)
- WIDTH OF HAT BETWEEN EARS: 2½ IN. (6 CM)

✺✺✺✺✺

SUPPLIES
- 40 YD (37 M) MEDIUM WEIGHT YARN IN A (PURPLE)
- 15 YD (14 M) MEDIUM WEIGHT YARN IN B (GREEN)
- SIZE 7 (4.5 MM) DPNS
- SIZE G6 (4 MM) CROCHET HOOK
- YARN NEEDLE
- POLYESTER FIBERFILL

YOUR CAT WILL BEWITCH AND BEGUILE IN THIS HAT, ESPECIALLY ON HALLOWEEN! HAVE FUN WITH THE

COLORS ON THIS PROJECT-USE A SPARKLY YARN FOR AN ESPECIALLY ENCHANTING LOOK.

WITCH

BASE
Using yarn A and two dpns, cast on 3 sts, leaving a 25 in. (64 cm) tail.
Row 1: Knit.
Row 2: Kfb, k to last st, kfb. (5 sts)
Rep last 2 rows five more times. (15 sts)
FIRST EAR HOLE
Row 13: K2, bind off next 11 sts, k last st.
Row 14: K2, cast on 11 sts, k2.
MIDDLE SECTION
Knit 16 rows.
SECOND EAR HOLE
Row 31: K2, bind off next 11 sts, k last st.
Row 32: K2, cast on 11 sts, k2.
Row 33: Knit.
Row 34: K2tog, k to last 2 sts, k2tog. (13 sts)
Rep last 2 rows five more times. (3 sts)
Bind off, leaving a 25 in. (64 cm) tail.

To create ties, use crochet hook and 25 in. (64 cm) tail, pull a loop through each stitch on bind off edge (3 loops), yo, pull one loop through, work 25ch, pull end through loop tightly, and snip extra yarn. Repeat with other 25 in. (64 cm) tail.

HAT
Using yarn B, cast on 30 sts, leaving a 15 in. (38 cm) tail. Distribute sts evenly across three dpns (10 sts per needle) and join to work in the round.
Rnds 1–3: Knit.
Change to yarn A.
Rnd 4: Knit.
Rnd 5: [K1, k2tog, k4, k2tog, k1] 3 times. (24 sts)
Rnds 6–8: Knit.

HAT: 3 IN. (7.5 CM) HIGH

FALL UNDER THE SPELL OF LINK, THE ENCHANTING BIRMAN.

Rnd 9: [K1, k2tog, k2, k2tog, k1] 3 times. (18 sts)
Rnds 10–12: Knit.
Rnd 13: [K1, k2tog x 2, k1] 3 times. (12 sts)
Rnds 14–16: Knit.
Rnd 17: K2tog around. (6 sts)
Rnds 18–20: Knit.
Cut yarn, leaving a 6 in. (15 cm) tail, and pull through loops on needle. If desired, run a hidden stitch ½ in. (1 cm) from the top of the hat and tug, to give the hat a rumpled look. Knot yarn on underside of hat to keep effect in place.

Using polyester fiberfill, lightly stuff hat. Do not overfill. Center the hat on the middle of the base and stitch into place using yarn B tail. Stitch along cast on edge of hat. Once finished, secure to underside of hat base.

METHOD: KNIT

SKILL LEVEL: DIFFICULT

Back to Hat Selector

SIZE

TO FIT AN AVERAGE ADULT CAT

- **EAR OPENING: 2½ IN. (6 CM)**
- **WIDTH OF HAT BETWEEN EARS: 2½ IN. (6 CM)**

✹✹✹✹✹

SUPPLIES

- **30 YD (27 M) WORSTED WEIGHT YARN IN A (LIGHT PINK)**
- **15 YD (14 M) WORSTED WEIGHT YARN IN B (HOT PINK)**
- **15 YD (14 M) WORSTED WEIGHT YARN IN C (WHITE)**
- **SIZE 7 (4.5 MM) DPNS**
- **SIZE G6 (4 MM) CROCHET HOOK**
- **YARN NEEDLE**
- **POLYESTER FIBERFILL**

AN ODE TO A FAVORITE TREAT! HAVE FUN WITH THE TOPPINGS ON YOUR "CUPCAKE!"

CUPCAKE

BASE
Using yarn A and two dpns, cast on 3 sts, leaving a 25 in. (64 cm) tail.
Row 1: Knit.
Row 2: Kfb, k to last st, kfb. (5 sts)
Rep last 2 rows five more times. (15 sts)

FIRST EAR HOLE
Row 13: K2, bind off next 11 sts, k last st.
Row 14: K2, cast on 11 sts, k2.

MIDDLE SECTION
Knit 16 rows.

SECOND EAR HOLE
Row 31: K2, bind off next 11 sts, k last st.
Row 32: K2, cast on 11 sts, k2.
Row 33: Knit.
Row 34: K2tog, k to last 2 sts, k2tog. (13 sts)
Rep last 2 rows five more times. (3 sts)
Bind off, leaving a 25 in. (64 cm) tail.

To create ties, use crochet hook and 25 in. (64 cm) tail, pull a loop through each stitch on bind off edge (3 loops), yo, pull one loop through, work 25ch, pull end through loop tightly, and snip extra yarn. Repeat with other 25 in. (64 cm) tail.

CUPCAKE WRAPPER
Using yarn B and two dpns, cast on 6 sts.
Knit 30 rows.
Bind off.
Sew ends together.
Weave tails to the bottom of the band.

CUPCAKE
Using yarn C, pick up 30 sts along edge of band. Place 10 sts on each of three dpns.
Knit 5 rnds.
Rnd 6: [K3, k2tog] to end. (24 sts)
Rnds 7–8: Knit.
Rnd 9: [K2, k2tog] to end. (18 sts)

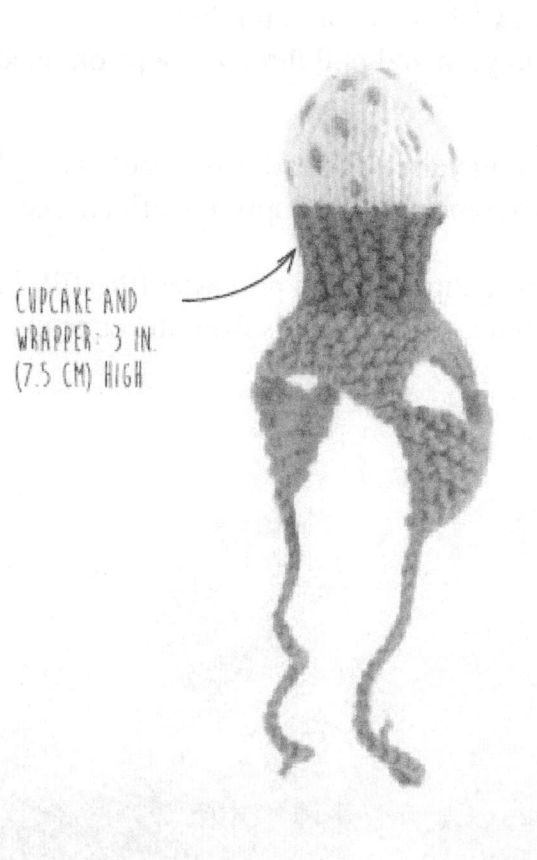

CUPCAKE AND WRAPPER: 3 IN. (7.5 CM) HIGH

Rnd 10: Knit.
Rnd 11: [K1, k2tog] to end. (12 sts)
Rnd 12: Knit.
Rnd 13: K2tog around. (6 sts)
Cut yarn and pull through loops on needles.

SPRINKLES
Using yarn A, thread yarn needle and sew short stitches on the white "frosting" in random spots for a sprinkle effect. Secure yarn to inside of cupcake.

Stuff cupcake with polyester fiberfill. Stitch cupcake to the base of the hat, slightly off center, using the tails from the cupcake wrapper.

METHOD: KNIT

SKILL LEVEL: DIFFICULT

Back to Hat Selector

SIZE

TO FIT AN AVERAGE ADULT CAT
- EAR OPENING: 2½ IN. (6 CM)
- WIDTH OF HAT BETWEEN EARS: 2½ IN. (6 CM)

✳✳✳✳✳

SUPPLIES

- 40 YD (37 M) BULKY WEIGHT YARN IN A (YELLOW)
- 3 YD (2.7 M) BULKY WEIGHT YARN IN B (BROWN)
- SIZE 7 (4.5 MM) DPNS
- SIZE G6 (4 MM) CROCHET HOOK
- YARN NEEDLE

GUS GOES TO EXTREME LENGTHS TO CAMOUFLAGE HIMSELF WHILE ON THE PROWL.

WHAT DOES YOUR CAT GO BANANAS FOR? THESE KITTIES ARE BANANAS FOR BANANA HATS!

BANANA

BASE
Using yarn A and two dpns, cast on 3 sts, leaving a 25 in. (64 cm) tail.
Row 1: Knit.

Row 2: Kfb, k to last st, kfb. (5 sts)
Rep last 2 rows five more times. (15 sts)

FIRST EAR HOLE

Row 13: K2, bind off next 11 sts, k last st.
Row 14: K2, cast on 11 sts, k2.

MIDDLE SECTION

Knit 16 rows.

SECOND EAR HOLE

Row 31: K2, bind off next 11 sts, k last st.
Row 32: K2, cast on 11 sts, k2.
Row 33: Knit.
Row 34: K2tog, k to last 2 sts, k2tog. (13 sts)
Rep last 2 rows five more times. (3 sts)
Bind off, leaving a 25 in. (64 cm) tail.

To create ties, use crochet hook and 25 in. (64 cm) tail, pull a loop through each stitch on bind off edge (3 loops), yo, pull one loop through, work 25ch, pull end through loop tightly, and snip extra yarn. Repeat with other 25 in. (64 cm) tail.

BANANA

Using yarn A, cast on 20 sts, leaving a 15 in. (38 cm) tail. Divide sts evenly onto three dpns and join to work in the round.

Rnds 1–6: Knit.
Rnd 7: K14, k2tog, k2, k2tog. (18 sts)
Rnds 8–12: Knit.
Rnd 13: K5, [k2tog] 2 times, k9. (16 sts)
Rnd 14: K4, [k2tog] 2 times, k6. (14 sts)
Rnd 15: K3, [k2tog] 2 times, k7. (12 sts)
Rnds 16–18: Knit.
Rnd 19: K2, [k2tog] 2 times, k6. (10 sts)
Rnd 20: Knit.
Rnd 21: K1, [k2tog] 2 times, k1, [k2tog] 2 times. (6 sts)
Change to yarn B.
Knit 4 rnds.
Cut yarn and pull through loops on needles.

ASSEMBLY

You should have a "flat side" to the banana—that side is the front. Stuff with polyester fiberfill, being mindful that the front should lay flat and the rest should curve. Use the blunt edge of a knitting needle to help stuff the stem of the banana if necessary. Attach to the middle of the base, centering the banana, and making sure the front of the banana is facing the front of the base (any side of the base can be the front). Using cast on tail, securely attach the banana to the hat base by stitching along the cast on edge of the banana. When finished, tie off to underside of base.

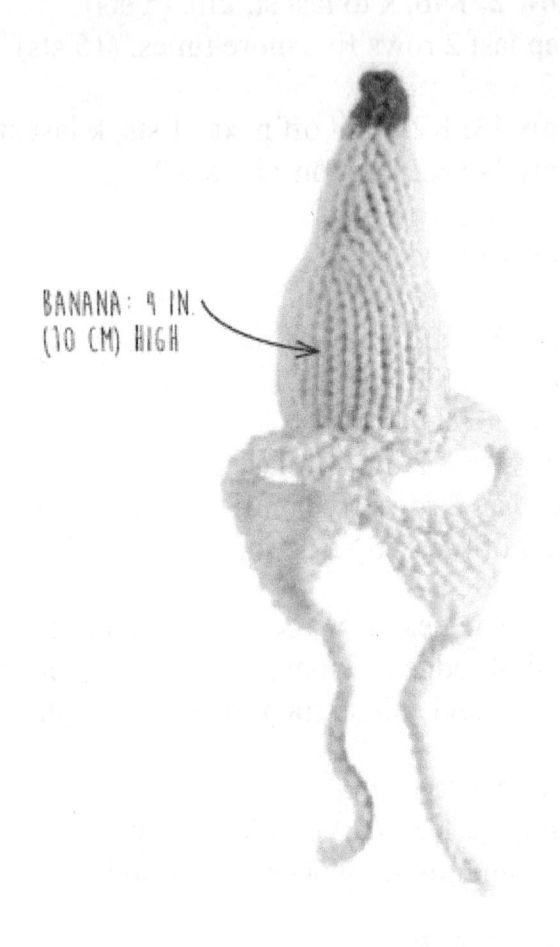

BANANA: 4 IN. (10 CM) HIGH

IF YOU'VE BEEN GOOD GIRLS AND BOYS, LINK MAY DELIVER YOUR CHRISTMAS PRESENTS.

METHOD: KNIT

SKILL LEVEL: DIFFICULT

Back to Hat Selector

SIZE
TO FIT AN AVERAGE ADULT CAT
- EAR OPENING: 2 IN. (5 CM)
- WIDTH OF HAT BETWEEN EARS: 2 IN. (5 CM)

❋❋❋❋❋

SUPPLIES
- 25 YD (23 M) BULKY WEIGHT YARN IN A (RED)
- 10 YD (9 M) BULKY WEIGHT YARN IN B (WHITE)
- SIZE 7 (4.5 MM) DPNS
- SIZE G6 (4 MM) CROCHET HOOK
- YARN NEEDLE
- POM POM MAKER (OPTIONAL)

A CLASSIC SANTA HAT, SLIGHTLY SLOUCHY AND KNIT IN RICH COLORS. ITS NOSTALGIC LOOK IS GREAT FOR

SEASONAL PHOTOS!

SANTA HAT

BASE
Using yarn A and two dpns, cast on 3 sts, leaving a 25 in. (64 cm) tail.
Row 1: Knit.
Row 2: Kfb, k to last st, kfb. (5 sts)
Rep last 2 rows five more times. (15 sts)
FIRST EAR HOLE
Row 13: K2, bind off next 11 sts, k last st.
Row 14: K2, cast on 11 sts, k2.
MIDDLE SECTION
Knit 16 rows.
SECOND EAR HOLE
Row 31: K2, bind off next 11 sts, k last st.
Row 32: K2, cast on 11 sts, k2.
Row 33: Knit.
Row 34: K2tog, k to last 2 sts, k2tog. (13 sts)
Rep last 2 rows five more times. (3 sts)
Bind off, leaving a 25 in. (64 cm) tail.

To create ties, use crochet hook and 25 in. (64 cm) tail, pull a loop through each stitch on bind off edge (3 loops), yo, pull one loop through, work 25ch, pull end through loop tightly, and snip extra yarn. Repeat with other 25 in. (64 cm) tail.

HAT
Using yarn A, cast on 30 sts, leaving a 25 in. (64 cm) tail. Divide sts evenly over three dpns (10 sts per needle). Being careful not to twist sts, join to work in the round.
Rnds 1–4: Knit.
Rnd 5: [K2tog, k6, k2tog] 3 times. (24 sts)
Rnds 6–9: Knit.
Rnd 10: [K2tog, k4, k2tog] 3 times. (18 sts)
Rnds 11–12: Knit.
Rnd 13: [K2tog, k2, k2tog] 3 times. (12 sts)
Rnds 14–15: Knit.
Rnd 16: [K2tog] 6 times. (6 sts)

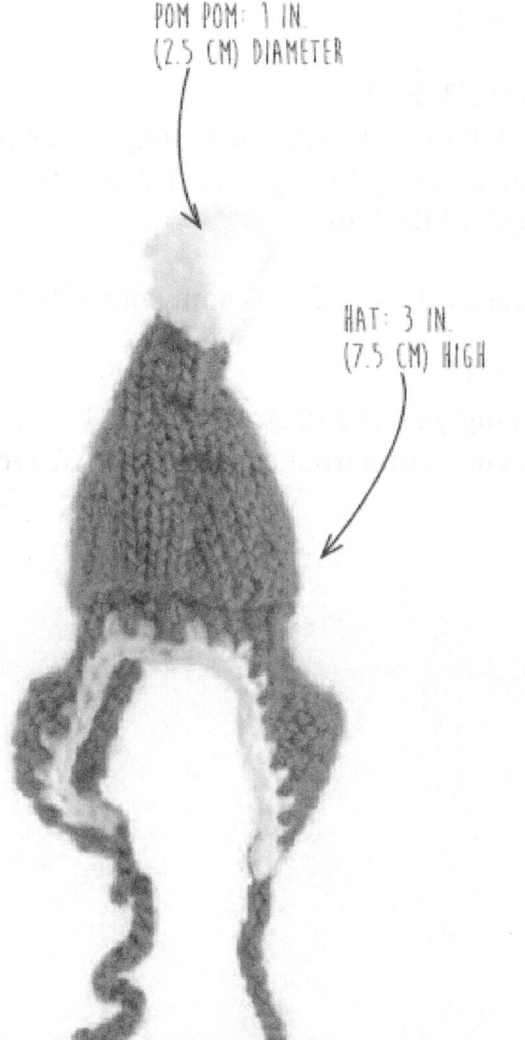

Rnd 17: Knit.
Rnd 18: [K2tog] 3 times. (3 sts)
Cut yarn, leaving a 10 in. (25 cm) tail. Pull through loops on needle and securely close top of hat.

To slouch hat, use the bind off tail and weave yarn through sts until yarn is about 1 in. (2.5 cm) from top. Tug until desired slouch is achieved. Knot yarn on inside to secure slouch.

ASSEMBLY
Stitch the hat to the base using the long cast on tail from the hat. Center the hat, and stitch evenly through the cast on edge. The hat should reach the edge of the front and back of the base.

Make a 1 in. (2.5 cm) pom pom with yarn B. Attach to the top of the hat.

TRIM
Using yarn B and crochet hook, begin on right side of base and work single crochet evenly along front edge of base. Weave in ends to the underside of hat base and secure.

WHO BETTER TO WISH YOUR FRIENDS AND FAMILY SEASON'S GREETINGS THAN DAISY?

METHOD: KNIT

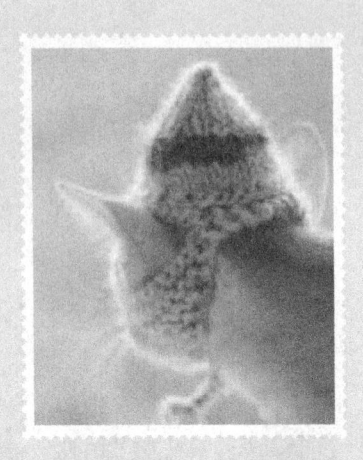

SKILL LEVEL: DIFFICULT

Back to Hat Selector

SIZE

TO FIT A SMALL ADULT CAT
- EAR OPENING: 2 IN. (5 CM)
- WIDTH OF HAT BETWEEN EARS: 2 IN. (5 CM)

✳✳✳✳✳

SUPPLIES

- 40 YD (37 M) BULKY WEIGHT YARN IN A (GREEN)
- 10 YD (9 M) BULKY WEIGHT YARN IN B (RED)
- SIZE 7 (4.5 MM) DPNS
- SIZE G6 (4 MM) CROCHET HOOK
- YARN NEEDLE
- POLYESTER FIBERFILL

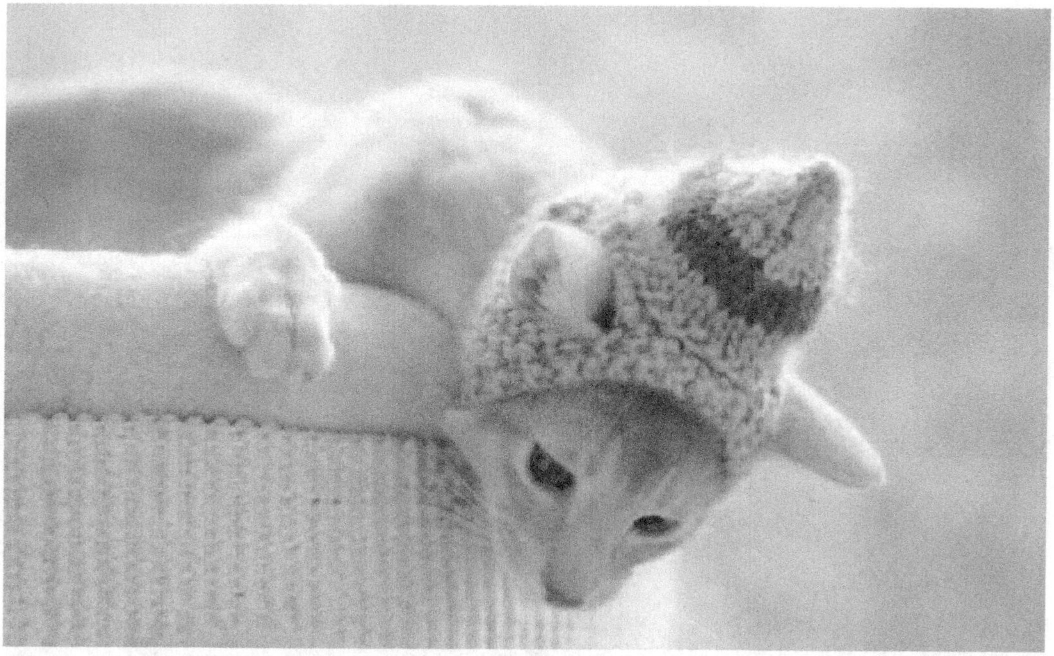

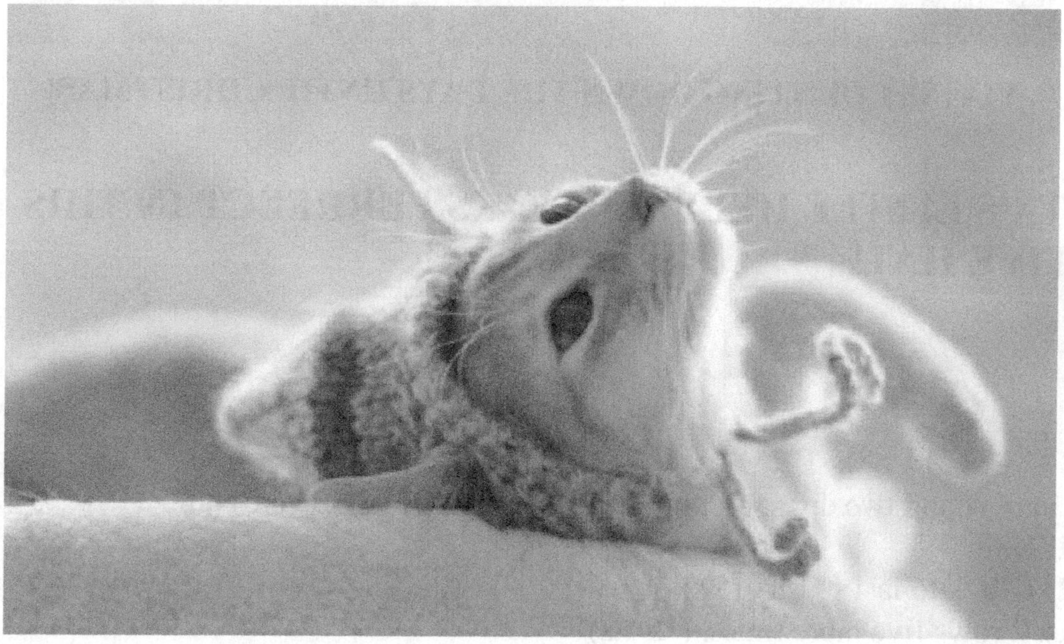

VIVI IS COUNTING DOWN THE DAYS UNTIL CHRISTMAS!

SANTA'S LITTLE HELPER LOOKS PURRFECT IN THIS FESTIVE HAT!

ELF

BASE
Using yarn A and two dpns, cast on 3 sts, leaving a 25 in. (64 cm) tail.
Row 1: Knit.
Row 2: Kfb, k to last st, kfb. (5 sts)
Rep last 2 rows five more times. (15 sts)

FIRST EAR HOLE
Row 13: K2, bind off next 11 sts, k last st.
Row 14: K2, cast on 11 sts, k2.

MIDDLE SECTION
Knit 16 rows.

SECOND EAR HOLE
Row 31: K2, bind off 11 next sts, k last st.
Row 32: K2, cast on 11 sts, k2.
Row 33: Knit.
Row 34: K2tog, k to last 2 sts, k2tog. (13 sts)

Rep last 2 rows five more times. (3 sts)
Bind off, leaving a 25 in. (64 cm) tail.

To create ties, use crochet hook and 25 in. (64 cm) tail, pull a loop through each stitch on bind off edge (3 loops), yo, pull one loop through, work 25ch, pull end through loop tightly, and snip extra yarn. Repeat with other 25 in. (64 cm) tail.

HAT

Using yarn A, cast on 30 sts, leaving a 15 in. (38 cm) tail. Divide sts evenly onto three dpns (10 sts per needle). Join to begin working in the round.

Rnds 1–3: Knit.
Change to yarn B.
Rnd 4: Knit.
Rnd 5: [K3, k2tog] around. (24 sts)
Rnd 6: Knit.
Change to yarn A.
Rnd 7: [K2, k2tog] around. (18 sts)
Rnd 8: Knit.
Rnd 9: [K1, k2tog] around. (12 sts)
Rnds 10–11: Knit.
Rnd 12: K2tog around. (6 sts)
Rnd 13: Knit.
Rnd 14: K2tog around. (3 sts)
Cut yarn and pull through loops. Lightly stuff hat with polyester fiberfill. Stitch to middle section of base using cast on tail from hat.

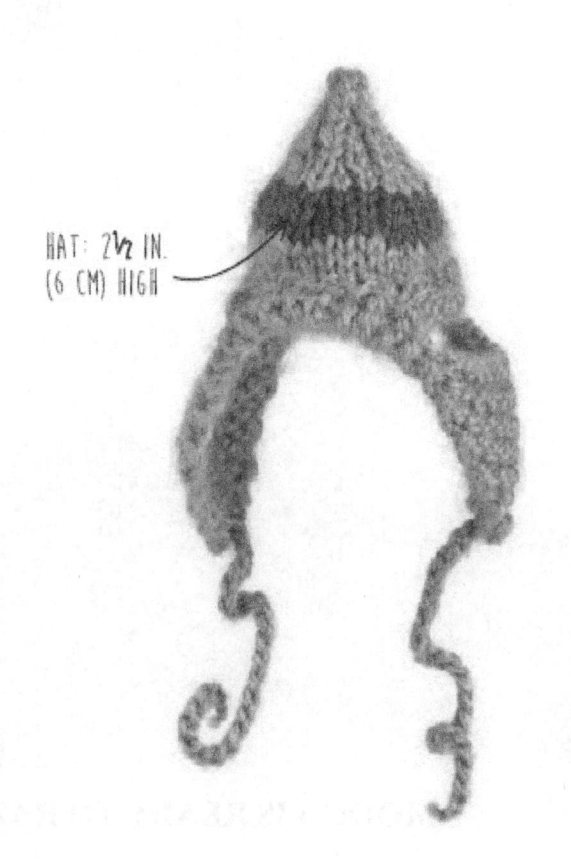

HAT: 2½ IN. (6 CM) HIGH

MOOCH IS READY TO RAZZLE DAZZLE IN HIS TOP HAT.

METHOD: KNIT

SKILL LEVEL: DIFFICULT

Back to Hat Selector

SIZE

TO FIT AN AVERAGE ADULT CAT
- EAR OPENING: 2 IN. (5 CM)
- WIDTH OF HAT BETWEEN EARS: 2½ IN. (6 CM)

✴✴✴✴✴

SUPPLIES

- 15 YD (14 M) WORSTED WEIGHT YARN IN A (BLACK)
- 45 YD (41 M) SPARKLY SPORT WEIGHT YARN IN B (BROWN)
- SIZE 7 (4.5 MM) DPNS
- POLYESTER FIBERFILL
- YARN NEEDLE
- SIZE 7 (4.5 MM) CROCHET HOOK
- ½ IN. (1 CM) WIDE BLACK SATIN RIBBON (OPTIONAL)

A CLASSIC TOP HAT FOR FANCY FELINES EVERYWHERE! A BIT OF SPARKLE MAKES THIS SUITABLE FOR SPECIAL

OCCASIONS OR RINGING IN A NEW YEAR!

TOP HAT

BASE
Using yarn A and two dpns, cast on 3 sts, leaving a 20 in. (51 cm) tail.
Row 1: Knit.
Row 2: Kfb, k to last st, kfb. (5 sts)
Rep last 2 rows three more times. (11 sts)
FIRST EAR HOLE
Row 9: K1, bind off next 9 sts.
Row 10: K1, cast on 9 sts, k1.
MIDDLE SECTION
Knit 16 rows.
SECOND EAR HOLE
Row 27: K1, bind off next 9 sts.
Row 28: K1, cast on 9 sts, k1.
Row 29: Knit.
Row 30: K2tog, k to last 2 sts, k2tog. (9 sts)
Rep last 2 rows three more times. (3 sts)
Bind off, leaving a 20 in. (51 cm) tail.

To create ties, use crochet hook and 20 in. (51 cm) tail, pull a loop through each stitch on bind off edge (3 loops), yo, pull one loop through, work 25ch, pull end through loop tightly, and snip extra yarn. Repeat with other 20 in. (51 cm) tail.

TOP HAT
TOP OF HAT
To get a flat top for the hat, you will be creating a flap that will need to be stitched into place later, so that the hat has a smooth top.
Using yarn B and two dpns, cast on 1 st, leaving a 4 in. (10 cm) tail.

Row 1: [K1, p1, k1] all into st. (3 sts)
Row 2: Purl.
Row 3: Kfb of all sts. (6 sts)
Row 4: Purl.
Row 3: Kfb of all sts. (12 sts)

Divide sts onto three dpns (4 sts per needle) and join to work in the round.
Next rnd: Knit.
Next rnd: [Kfb, k1] around. (18 sts)
Next rnd: Knit.
Next rnd: [Kfb, k2] around. (24 sts)
Next rnd: Knit.
Next rnd: [Kfb, k3] around. (30 sts)
Next rnd: Purl.

TUBE OF HAT
Knit 15 rnds.
Bind off, leaving a 20 in. (51 cm) tail. Using the cast on tail, stitch the flap created on the top of the hat into place, so that it lies flat. Next, using the 20 in. (51 cm) tail, begin stitching the top hat in place on the base of the cat hat. Center the top hat on the middle section of the base, stitching into the bind off edge of the top hat. Once you have stitched halfway around the hat, lightly stuff the hat with polyester fiberfill. Overstuffing will give the wrong shape. Continue stitching around the bind off edge of the hat until it is securely in place. Weave in ends of hat securely on underside of the base and snip.

BRIM
Using yarn B and two dpns, cast on 6 sts, leaving a 4 in. (10 cm) tail. Knit every row until band measures 9 in. (23 cm). Bind off, leaving a 20 in. (51 cm) tail. Stitch ends of the brim together using cast on tail. Weave in tail and snip. Slide the brim over the top hat, to the bottom of the top hat. Using the 20 in. (51 cm) tail, stitch the brim onto the base of the hat, following along the bind off edge of the top hat. When finished, pull end through the underside of the cat hat base, weave in securely, and snip.

Once stitched into place, use a length of yarn B and a yarn needle to create some simple stitches that will anchor the brim into the appropriate shape. The brim will naturally roll, though you want the front to be flat. You can place a few small stitches on each side of the front brim, to secure the roll and keep the front flat. Weave in any ends to underside of the base and snip.

Measure ribbon around the bottom of the hat, add 1 in. (2.5 cm), and cut. Fold one end over ½ in. (1.25 cm), then fold over ½ in. (1.25 cm) again. Using matching thread and a needle, stitch this fold into place. Wrap the ribbon around the bottom of hat, secure raw end under the fold, and stitch in place to create the band.

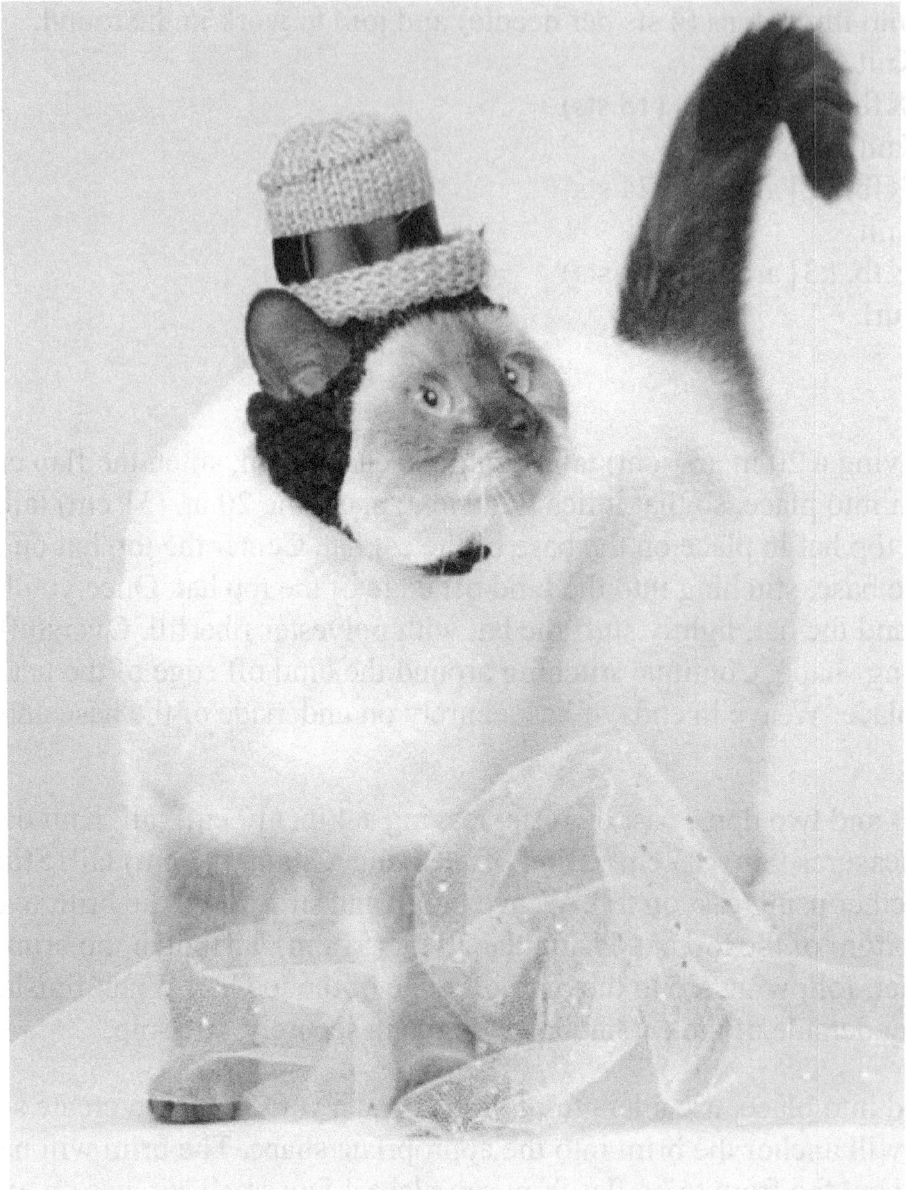

METHOD: CROCHET

SKILL LEVEL: BEGINNER

Back to Hat Selector

SIZE

TO FIT A SMALL ADULT CAT
- EAR OPENING: 2 IN. (5 CM)
- WIDTH OF HAT BETWEEN EARS: 2 IN. (5 CM)

✳✳✳✳✳

SUPPLIES

- 20 YD (18 M) WORSTED WEIGHT YARN IN A (PINK)
- 5 YD (4.5 M) WORSTED WEIGHT YARN IN B (GREEN)
- SIZE H8 (5 MM) CROCHET HOOK
- YARN NEEDLE
- POM POM MAKER (OPTIONAL)

THIS PEPPY POM POM HAT IS THE PERFECT ACCESSORY FOR ANY HIGH-SPIRITED KITTY.

POM POM HAT

BASE
Using yarn A, work 2ch, leaving a 25 in. (64 cm) tail.
Row 1: 3sc in 2nd ch, 1ch.
Row 2: 3sc, 1ch.
Row 3: 2sc in first st, 1sc, 2sc in last st, 1ch. (5sc)
Row 4: 5sc, 1ch.
Row 5: 2sc in first st, 3sc, 2sc in last st, 1ch. (7sc)
Row 6: 7sc, 1ch.
Row 7: 2sc in first st, 5sc, 2sc in last st, 1ch. (9sc)
Row 8: 9sc, 1ch.
Row 9: 2sc in first st, 7sc, 2sc in last st, 1ch. (11sc)

FIRST EAR HOLE
Row 10: 1sc, 9ch, 1sc in last st, 1ch.

MIDDLE SECTION
Rows 11–20: 11sc, 1ch.

SECOND EAR HOLE
Row 21: 1sc, 9ch, 1sc in last st, 1ch.
Row 22: 11sc, 1ch.
Row 23: 1sc, skip next st, 7sc, skip next st, 1sc, 1ch. (9sc)
Row 24: 9sc, 1ch.
Row 25: 1sc, skip next st, 5sc, skip next st, 1sc, 1ch. (7sc)
Row 26: 7sc, 1ch.
Row 27: 1sc, skip next st, 3sc, skip next st, 1sc, 1ch. (5sc)
Row 28: 5sc, 1ch.
Row 29: 1sc, skip next st, 1sc, skip next st, 1sc, 1ch. (3sc)
Row 30: 3sc, 1ch.
Row 31: 1sc in last st.

POM POM:
1 IN. (2.5 CM) DIAMETER

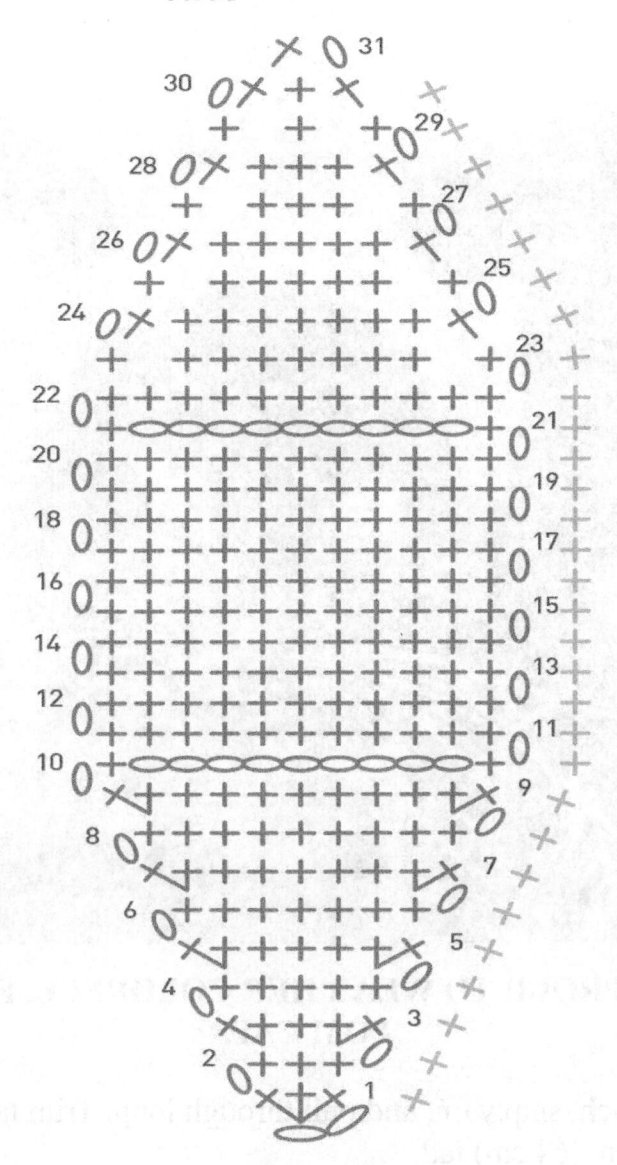

BASE

○ ch
+ sc

RACHEL IS PROUD TO WEAR HER COLORFUL, FLUFFY POM POM CAP.

To create ties, work 25ch, snip yarn, and pull through loop. Trim tail. Work 25ch at the beg of base, using 25 in. (64 cm) tail.

FRONT TRIM
Holding yarns A and B together, work 30sc across front of hat base. Clip yarn, pull through loop, and fasten securely on underside of the hat.

Make a 1 in. (2.5 cm) pom pom from yarns A and B and attach to center of hat.

This is an easy design to adapt. Use your favorite sports team colors or holiday colors to make it your own.

FOR THE LITTLE LION WHO THINKS HE'S A BIG ONE!

METHOD: CROCHET

SKILL LEVEL: BEGINNER

Back to Hat Selector

SIZE

TO FIT AN AVERAGE ADULT CAT
- EAR OPENING: 2½ IN. (6 CM)
- WIDTH OF HAT BETWEEN EARS: 2½ IN. (6 CM)

✳✳✳✳✳

SUPPLIES
- 30 YD (27 M) WORSTED WEIGHT YARN IN A (LIGHT ORANGE)
- 30 YD (27 M) WORSTED WEIGHT YARN IN B (DARK ORANGE)
- SIZE G6 (4 MM) CROCHET HOOK
- SIZE E4 (3.5 MM) CROCHET HOOK
- YARN NEEDLE

LITTLE LION

BASE
Using yarn A and size G6 (4 mm) hook, work 2ch, leaving a 25 in. (64 cm) tail.
Row 1: 3sc in 2nd ch, 1ch.

Row 2: 3sc, 1ch.
Row 3: 2sc in first st, 1sc, 2sc in last st, 1ch. (5sc)
Row 4: 5sc, 1ch.
Row 5: 2sc in first st, 3sc, 2sc in last st, 1ch. (7sc)
Row 6: 7sc, 1ch.
Row 7: 2sc in first st, 5sc, 2sc in last st, 1ch. (9sc)
Row 8: 9sc, 1ch.
Row 9: 2sc in first st, 7sc, 2sc in last st, 1ch. (11sc)
Row 10: 11sc, 1ch.
Row 11: 2sc in first st, 9sc, 2sc in last st, 1ch. (13sc)
Row 12: 13sc, 1ch.
Row 13: 2sc in first st, 11sc, 2sc in last st, 1ch. (15sc)

FIRST EAR HOLE
Row 14: 1sc, 13ch, 1sc in last st, 1ch.

MIDDLE SECTION
Rows 15–26: 15sc, 1ch.

SECOND EAR HOLE
Row 27: 1sc, 13ch, 1sc in last st, 1ch.
Row 28: 15sc, 1ch.
Row 29: 1sc, skip next st, 11sc, skip next st, 1sc, 1ch. (13sc)
Row 30: 13sc, 1ch.
Row 31: 1sc, skip next st, 9sc, skip next st, 1sc, 1ch. (11sc)

Row 32: 11sc, 1ch.
Row 33: 1sc, skip next st, 7sc, skip next st, 1sc, 1ch. (9sc)
Row 34: 9sc, 1ch.
Row 35: 1sc, skip next st, 5sc, skip next st, 1sc, 1ch. (7sc)
Row 36: 7sc, 1ch.
Row 37: 1sc, skip next st, 3sc, skip next st, 1sc, 1ch. (5sc)
Row 38: 5sc, 1ch.
Row 39: 1sc, skip next st, 1sc, skip next st, 1sc, 1ch. (3sc)
Row 40: 1sc in last st. Work 25ch, snip yarn, and pull through loop tightly.
Trim tail. Work 25ch at beg of base, using 25 in. (64 cm) tail.

MANE

Using yarn B and size E4 (3.5 mm) crochet hook, work the mane evenly along the front edge of the hat base. Starting just above the right tie:
Row 1: [Sl st in next sp, 8ch, sl st in same sp] rep across hat, making 40 loops.
Turn work. You will now work on top of the hat base, creating a second row of slightly larger loops.
Row 2: [Sl st in next sp, 12ch, sl st in same sp] rep across hat, making 40 loops and ending on the side the mane started on.

ASSEMBLY
Pull all ends to underside of hat and secure in place.

MANE: 2 ROWS OF 40 LOOPS

BASE

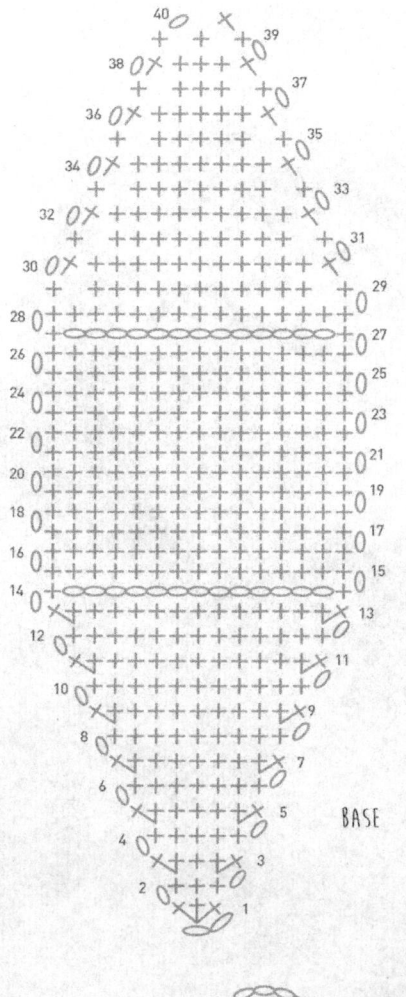

MANE ROW 1

MANE ROW 2

○ ch
• sl st
+ sc

WATCH OUT! POPPY IS ON THE PROWL.

METHOD: CROCHET

SKILL LEVEL: INTERMEDIATE

Back to Hat Selector

SIZE

TO FIT AN AVERAGE ADULT CAT
- EAR OPENING: 2 IN. (5 CM)
- WIDTH OF HAT BETWEEN EARS: 2½ IN. (6 CM)

✳✳✳✳✳

SUPPLIES

- 30 YD (27 M) WORSTED WEIGHT YARN IN A (ORANGE)
- 10 YD (9 M) WORSTED WEIGHT YARN IN B (WHITE)
- 3 YD (2.7 M) BULKY WEIGHT YARN IN C (BLACK)
- SIZE G6 (4 MM) CROCHET HOOK
- SIZE E4 (3.5 MM) CROCHET HOOK
- YARN NEEDLE

A CRAFTY HAT FOR YOUR CUNNING CAT! CHICKENS BEWARE!

FELINE FOX

BASE
Using yarn A and size G6 (4 mm) hook, work 2ch, leaving a 25 in. (64 cm) tail.
Row 1: 3sc in 2nd ch, 1ch.
Row 2: 3sc, 1ch.
Row 3: 2sc in first st, 1sc, 2sc in last st, 1ch. (5sc)
Row 4: 5sc, 1ch.
Row 5: 2sc in first st, 3sc, 2sc in last st, 1ch. (7sc)
Row 6: 7sc, 1ch.
Row 7: 2sc in first st, 5sc, 2sc in last st, 1ch. (9sc)
Row 8: 9sc, 1ch.
Row 9: 2sc in first st, 7sc, 2sc in last st, 1ch. (11sc)
Row 10: 11sc, 1ch.
Row 11: 2sc in first st, 9sc, 2sc in last st, 1ch. (13sc)

FIRST EAR HOLE
Row 12: 1sc, 11ch, 1sc in last st, 1ch.

MIDDLE SECTION
Rows 13–15: 13sc, 1ch.
Row 16: 2sc in first st, sc to end, 1ch. (14sc)
(The increase side is the front of the hat.)
Row 17: 13sc, 2sc in last st, 1ch. (15sc)
Row 18: 2sc in first st, sc to end, 1ch. (16sc)
Row 19: 15sc, 2sc in last st, 1ch. (17sc)
Row 20: Skip first st, 16sc, 1ch. (16sc)
Row 21: 14sc, skip next st, 1sc in last st, 1ch. (15sc)
Row 22: Skip first st, 14sc, 1ch. (14sc)
Row 23: 12sc, skip next st, 1sc in last st, 1ch. (13sc)
Rows 24–26: 13sc, 1ch.

DOMINO HAS A FANTASTIC FOXY MAKEOVER.

SECOND EAR HOLE
Row 27: 1sc, 11ch, 1sc in last st, 1ch.
Row 28: 13sc, 1ch.
Row 29: 1sc, skip next st, 9sc, skip next st, 1sc, 1ch. (11sc)
Row 30: 11sc, 1ch.
Row 31: 1sc, skip next st, 7sc, skip next st, 1sc, 1ch. (9sc)
Row 32: 9sc, 1ch.
Row 33: 1sc, skip next st, 5sc, skip next st, 1sc, 1ch. (7sc)
Row 34: 7sc, 1ch.
Row 35: 1sc, skip next st, 3sc, skip next st, 1sc, 1ch. (5sc)
Row 36: 5sc, 1ch.

Row 37: 1sc, skip next st, 1sc, skip next st, 1sc, 1ch. (3sc)
Row 38: 3sc, 1ch.
Row 39: 1sc in last st.

To create ties, work 25ch, snip yarn, and pull through loop tightly. Trim tail. Work 25ch at beg of base, using 25 in. (64 cm) tail.

OUTER EARS
(Make 2)
Using yarn A and size E4 (3.5 mm) hook, work 3ch.
Row 1: Skip first ch, 2sc, 1ch.
Row 2: 2sc, 1ch.
Row 3: 2sc in each st, 1ch. (4sc)
Row 4: 4sc, 1ch.
Row 5: 2sc in first st, 2sc, 2sc in last st, 1ch. (6sc)
Row 6: 6sc, 1ch.
Row 7: 2sc in first st, 4sc, 2sc in last st, 1ch. (8sc)
Row 8: 8sc, 1ch.
Row 9: 2sc in first st, 6sc, 2sc in last st, 1ch. (10sc)
Rows 10–11: 10sc, 1ch.
Cut a 10 in. (25 cm) tail and pull through loop.
Weave in other tail at point of ear.

INNER EARS
(Make 2)
Using yarn B and size E4 (3.5 mm) hook, work 3ch.
Row 1: Skip first ch, 2sc, 1ch.
Row 2: 2sc, 1ch.
Row 3: 2sc in each st, 1ch. (4sc)
Row 4: 4sc, 1ch.
Row 5: 2sc in first st, 2sc, 2sc in last st, 1ch. (6sc)
Rows 6–7: 6sc, 1ch.
Cut yarn, leaving a 10 in. (25 cm) tail, and pull through loop. Weave in other tail at point of ear.
Using yarn C and size E4 (3.5 mm) hook, work 5 sl sts along upper tip and point of inner ear. Weave in ends to WS of ear, and clip.

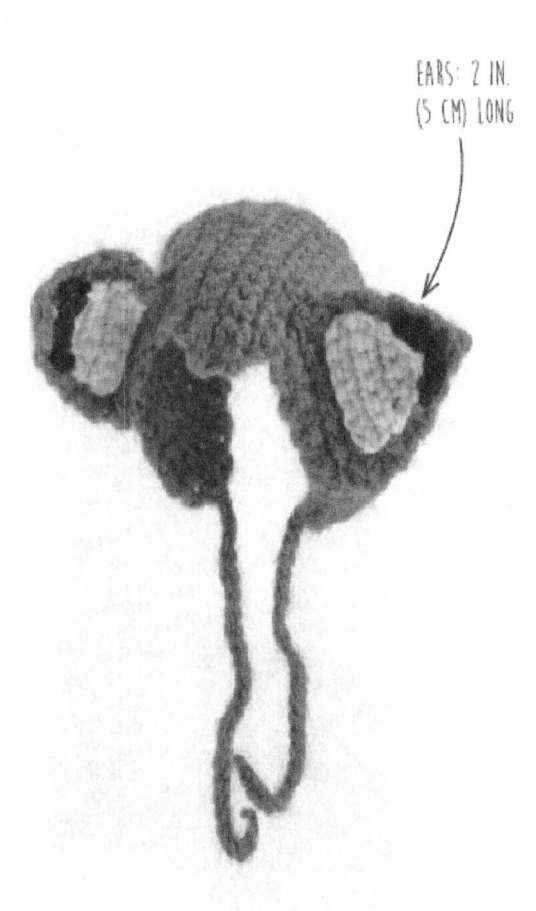

Attach one inner ear to one outer ear using the inner ear 10 in. (25 cm) tail and a yarn needle. Stitch into place, with the base of the ears (the last rows) matching up. Use the photos for reference if necessary. Be careful not to stitch right through the outer ear, as you do not want your stitches to be visible. You can create an invisible stitch by running your needle through the edge of the inner ear and barely through the surface of the outer ear.

ASSEMBLY

Stitch each ear along the front edge of the hat base, in front of each ear hole. The front edge of the base is the pointed edge. Use the yarn tails from the outer ears to stitch into place, running your needle through the edge of the outer ear. The ears are meant to stand up, so you may have to reinforce your stitches to give the ears support.

Stand back and admire your cat's new look!

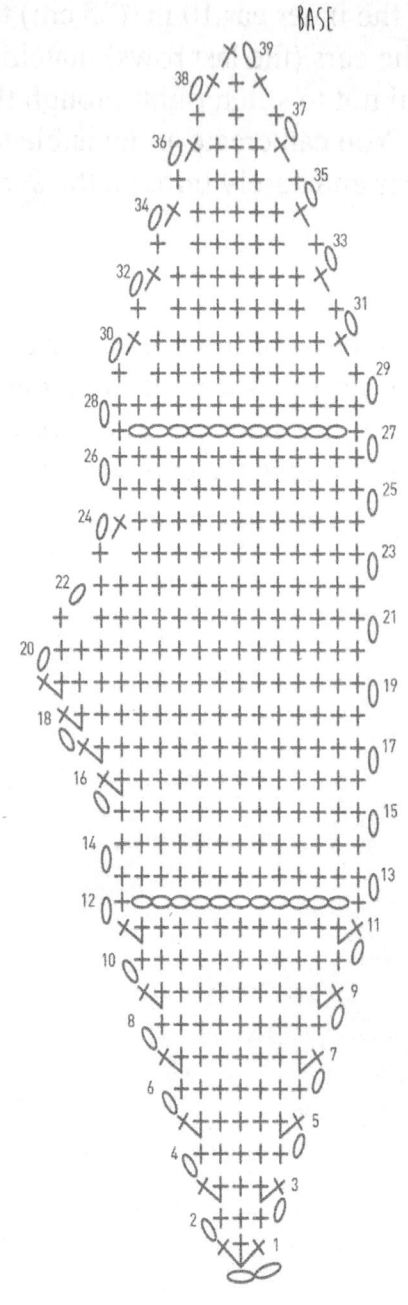

BASE

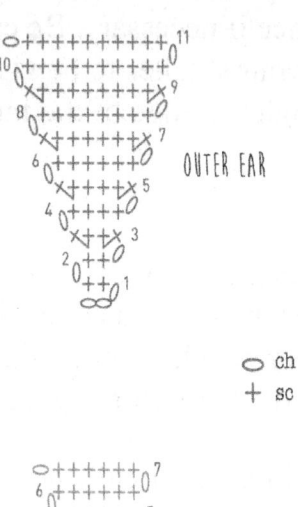

OUTER EAR

○ ch
+ sc

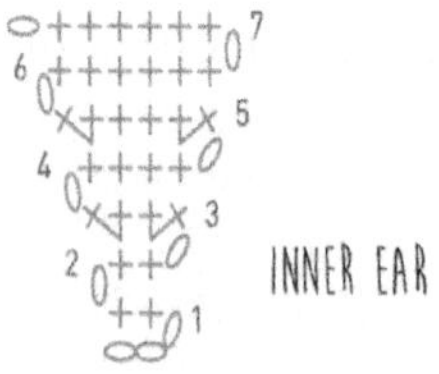

INNER EAR

130

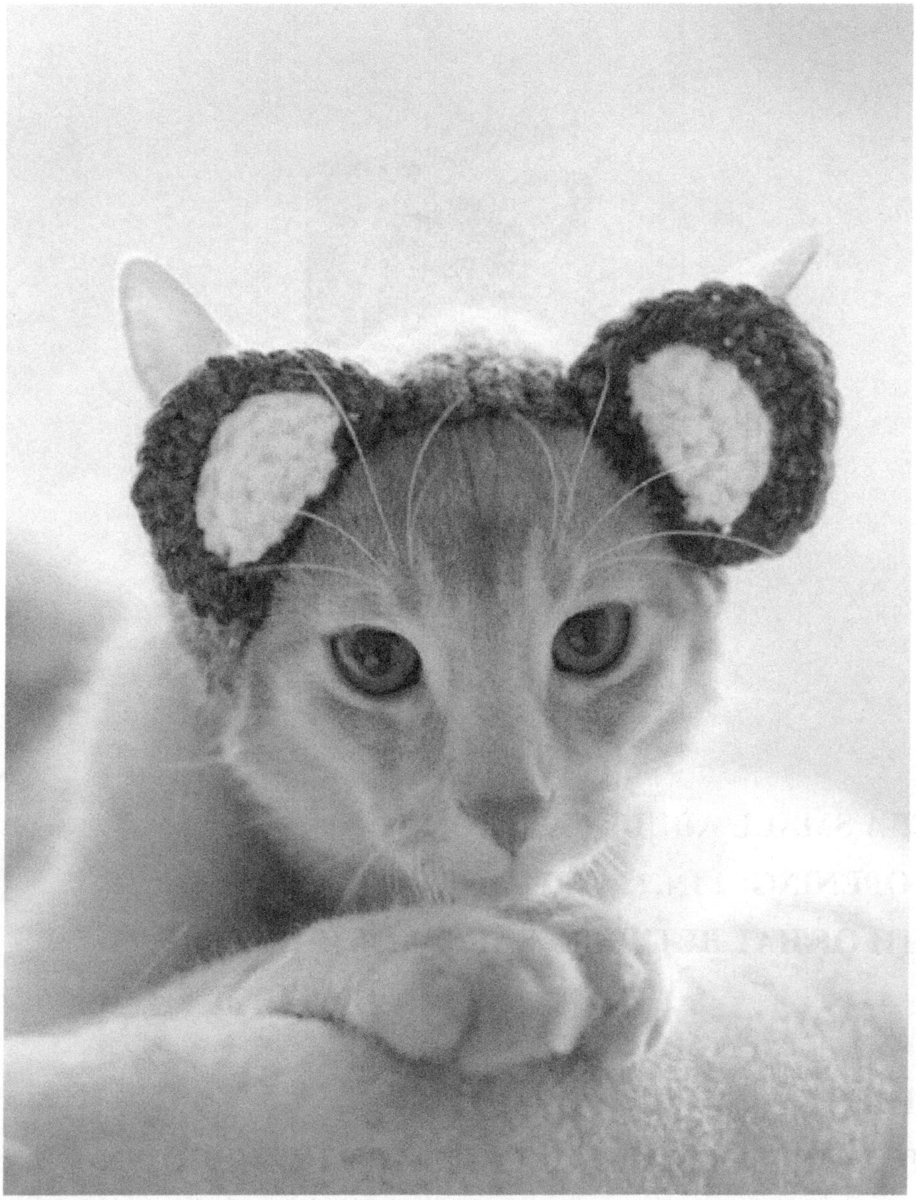

METHOD: CROCHET

SKILL LEVEL: INTERMEDIATE

Back to Hat Selector

SIZE

TO FIT A SMALL ADULT CAT
- EAR OPENING: 2 IN. (5 CM)
- WIDTH OF HAT BETWEEN EARS: 2 IN. (5 CM)

✳✳✳✳✳

SUPPLIES

- 25 YD (23 M) WORSTED WEIGHT YARN IN A (BROWN)
- 10 YD (9 M) WORSTED WEIGHT YARN IN B (WHITE)
- SIZE G6 (4 MM) CROCHET HOOK
- YARN NEEDLE

TRANSFORM YOUR KITTY INTO A CUDDLY TEDDY WITH THIS ADORABLE BEAR HAT.

BABY BEAR

BASE

Using yarn A, work 2ch, leaving a 25 in. (64 cm) tail.
Row 1: 3sc in 2nd ch, 1ch.
Row 2: 3sc, 1ch.
Row 3: 2sc in first st, 1sc, 2sc in last st, 1ch. (5sc)
Row 4: 5sc, 1ch.
Row 5: 2sc in first st, 3sc, 2sc in last st, 1ch. (7sc)
Row 6: 7sc, 1ch.
Row 7: 2sc in first st, 5sc, 2sc in last st, 1ch. (9sc)
Row 8: 9sc, 1ch.
Row 9: 2sc in first st, 7sc, 2sc in last st, 1ch. (11sc)
Row 10: 11sc, 1ch.
Row 11: 2sc in first st, 9sc, 2sc in last st, 1ch. (13sc)

FIRST EAR HOLE
Row 12: 1sc, 11ch, 1sc in last st, 1ch.

MIDDLE SECTION
Rows 13–22: 13sc, 1ch.

SECOND EAR HOLE
Row 23: 1sc, 11ch, 1sc in last st, 1ch.
Row 24: 13sc, 1ch.
Row 25: 1sc, skip next st, 9sc, skip next st, 1sc, 1ch. (11sc)
Row 26: 11sc, 1ch.
Row 27: 1sc, skip next st, 7sc, skip next st, 1sc, 1ch. (9sc)
Row 28: 9sc, 1ch.

Row 29: 1sc, skip next st, 5sc, skip next st, 1sc, 1ch. (7sc)
Row 30: 7sc, 1ch.
Row 31: 1sc, skip next st, 3sc, skip next st, 1sc, 1ch. (5sc)
Row 32: 5sc, 1ch.
Row 33: 1sc, skip next st, 1sc, skip next st, 1sc, 1ch. (3sc)
Row 34: 3sc, 1ch.
Row 35: 1sc in last st.

To create ties, work 25ch, snip yarn, and pull through loop tightly. Trim tail. Work 25ch at beg of base, using 25 in. (64 cm) tail.

OUTER EARS
(Make 2)
Using yarn A, work 2ch.
Row 1: 2sc in 2nd ch.
Row 2: 2sc in each st. (4sc)
Row 3: 2sc in each st. (8sc)
Row 4: 2sc, 2sc in next 4 sts, 2sc. (12sc)

Row 5: 4sc, 2sc in next 4 sts, 4sc. (16sc)
Cut a 10 in. (25 cm) tail and pull through loop.

INNER EARS
(Make 2)
Using yarn B, work 2ch.
Row 1: 2sc in 2nd ch.
Row 2: 2sc in each st. (4sc)
Row 3: 1sc, 2sc in next 2 sts, 1sc in last st. (6sc)
Cut a 10 in. (25 cm) tail and pull through loop. Attach to outer ear, lining up the bottom edge of the inner ear to the bottom edge of the outer ear. Be careful as you stitch around inner ear not to stitch all the way through the outer ear, as you don't want the yarn B stitches visible on the back of the outer ear. Repeat with other ear.

ASSEMBLY
Attach the ears along the front edge of the hat base, centered in front of each ear hole. Use the tail from the outer ear to stitch the ears into place. You may need to reinforce your stitches, as the ears are meant to stand up.

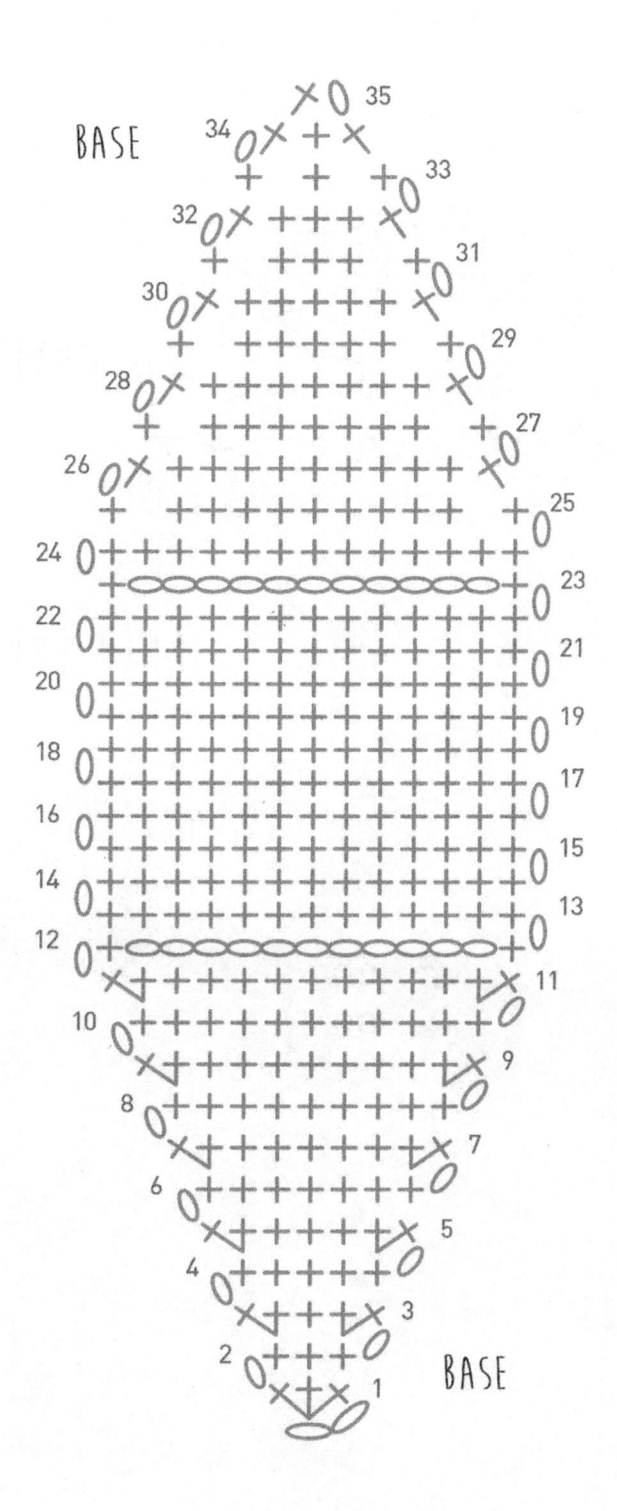

BASE

OUTER EAR

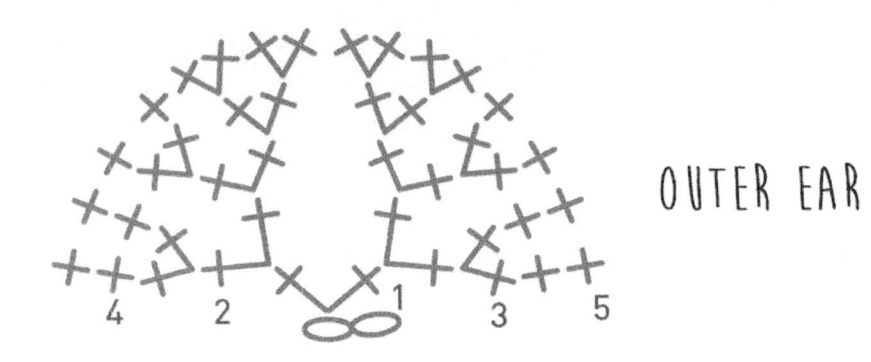

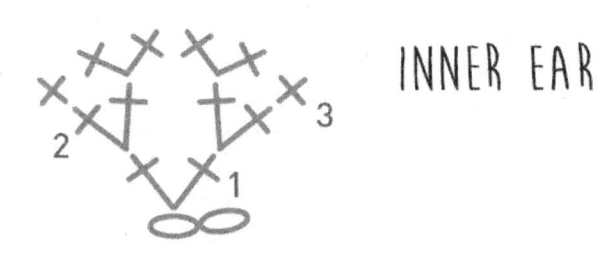

INNER EAR

○ ch
+ sc

137

METHOD: CROCHET

SKILL LEVEL: INTERMEDIATE

Back to Hat Selector

SIZE

TO FIT AN AVERAGE ADULT CAT
- **EAR OPENING: 2 IN. (5 CM)**
- **WIDTH OF HAT BETWEEN EARS: 2 IN. (5 CM)**

❊❊❊❊❊

SUPPLIES

- **40 YD (37 M) WORSTED WEIGHT YARN IN A (WHITE)**
- **20 YD (18 M) WORSTED WEIGHT YARN IN B (BROWN)**
- **SIZE G6 (4 MM) CROCHET HOOK**
- **YARN NEEDLE**

THE PERFECT PROJECT FOR DOG- AND CAT-LOVERS! CUSTOMIZE THE SPOTS, EARS, AND COLORS FOR DIFFERENT PUPS.

WHO SAYS CATS AND DOGS CAN'T GET ALONG? NOT DOMINO!

DOG

BASE
Using yarn A, work 2ch, leaving a 25 in. (64 cm) tail.
Row 1: 3sc in 2nd ch, 1ch.
Row 2: 3sc, 1ch.
Row 3: 2sc in first st, 1sc, 2sc in last st, 1ch. (5sc)
Row 4: 5sc, 1ch.
Row 5: 2sc in first st, 3sc, 2sc in last st, 1ch. (7sc)

Row 6: 7sc, 1ch.
Row 7: 2sc in first st, 5sc, 2sc in last st, 1ch. (9sc)
Row 8: 9sc, 1ch.
Row 9: 2sc in first st, 7sc, 2sc in last st, 1ch. (11sc)
Row 10: 11sc, 1ch.
Row 11: 2sc in first st, 9sc, 2sc in last st, 1ch. (13sc)
Row 12: 13sc, 1ch.
Row 13: 2sc in first st, 11sc, 2sc in last st, 1ch. (15sc)

FIRST EAR HOLE
Row 14: 1sc, 13ch, 1sc in last st, 1ch.

MIDDLE SECTION
Rows 15–26: 15sc, 1ch.

SECOND EAR HOLE
Row 27: 1sc, 13ch, 1sc in last st, 1ch.
Row 28: 15sc, 1ch.
Row 29: 1sc, skip next st, 11sc, skip next st, 1sc, 1ch. (13sc)
Row 30: 13sc, 1ch.

Row 31: 1sc, skip next st, 9sc, skip next st, 1sc, 1ch. (11sc)
Row 32: 11sc, 1ch.
Row 33: 1sc, skip next st, 7sc, skip next st, 1sc, 1ch. (9sc)
Row 34: 9sc, 1ch.
Row 35: 1sc, skip next st, 5sc, skip next st, 1sc, 1ch. (7sc)
Row 36: 7sc, 1ch.
Row 37: 1sc, skip next st, 3sc, skip next st, 1sc, 1ch. (5sc)
Row 38: 5sc, 1ch.
Row 39: 1sc, skip next st, 1sc, skip next st, 1sc, 1ch. (3sc)
Row 40: 1sc in last st.

To create ties, work 25ch, snip yarn, and pull through loop tightly. Trim tail. Work 25ch at beg of base, using 25 in. (64 cm) tail.

EARS
(Make 2)
Using yarn B, make a magic ring.
Rnd 1: 1ch, 10sc in ring.

EARS: 2 IN. (5 CM) LONG

Rnd 2: 10sc, 1ch.
Rnd 3: [1sc, 2sc in next st] 5 times, 1ch. (15sc)
Rnd 4: 15sc, 1ch.
Rnd 5: Working in back loops only, work 8sc, 1ch, turn.
Continue in rows:
Rows 6–11: 8sc, 1ch.
Cut a 10 in. (25 cm) tail and pull through loop. Weave in beg tail.

SPOTS
(Make 1 in A, 1 in B)
Work 6ch.
Rnd 1: 1sc in 2nd ch, 1sc in next 2ch, 2sc in next ch. Continuing along other side of chain, work 1sc in back loop of next 4ch, sl st to beg sc, 1ch.
Rnd 2: [1sc, 2sc in next st] 3 times, 2sc, 2sc in next st, sl st to beg sc (13sc). Cut a 6 in. (15 cm) tail and pull through loop. Weave in beg tail.

ASSEMBLY
To attach ears, use 10 in. (25 cm) tail to stitch flat side of ear evenly above ear opening on base of hat. Once securely stitched in place, pull tail through to underside of hat and secure. Repeat with other tail.

To attach spots, attach spot in yarn A to one ear. Stitch around spot securely, and pull end through to WS of ear. Secure. Attach spot in yarn B to base of hat, underneath the other ear.

EAR

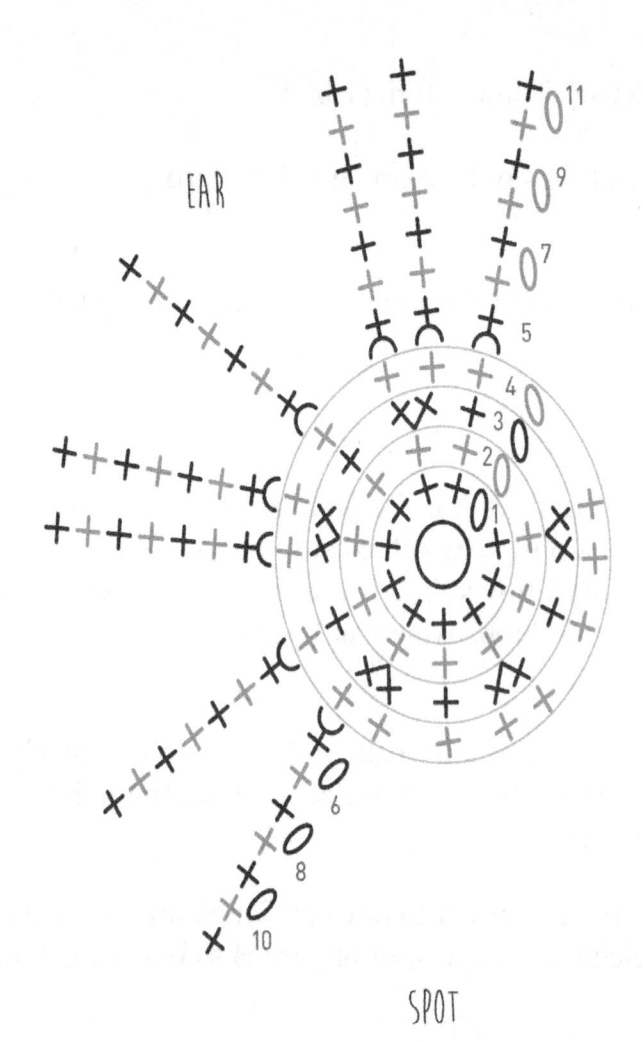

SPOT

○ ch
• sl st
+ sc
⋈ sc in back loops only

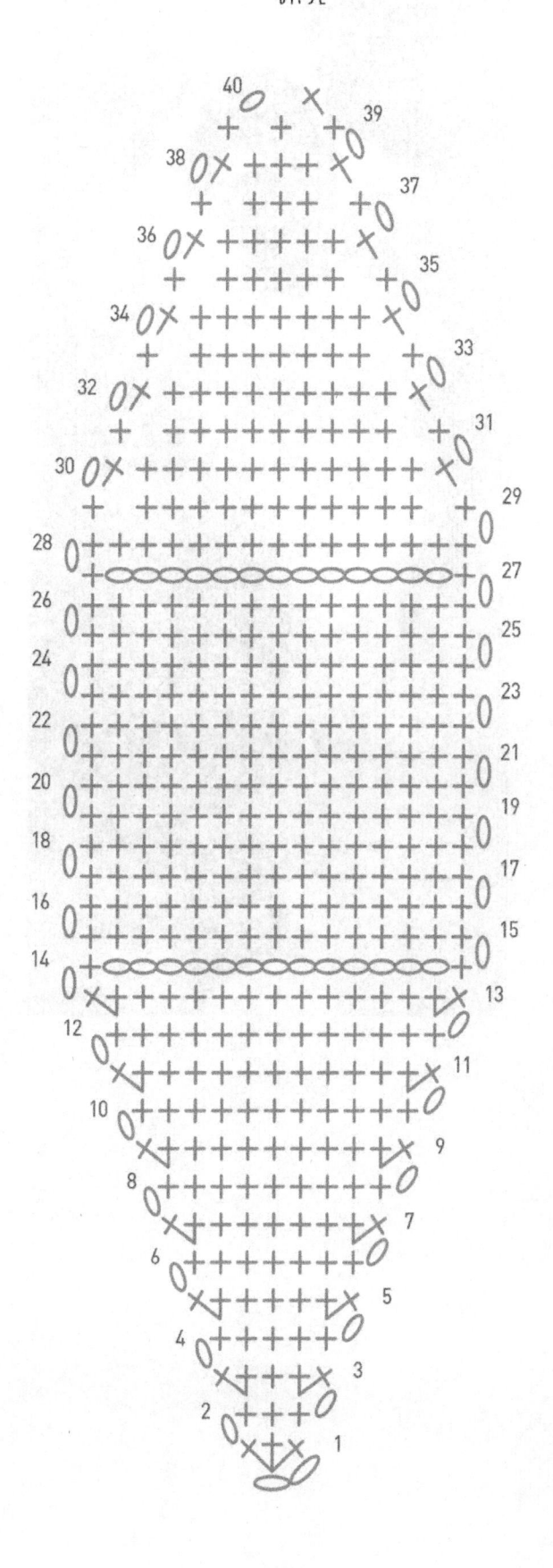

BASE

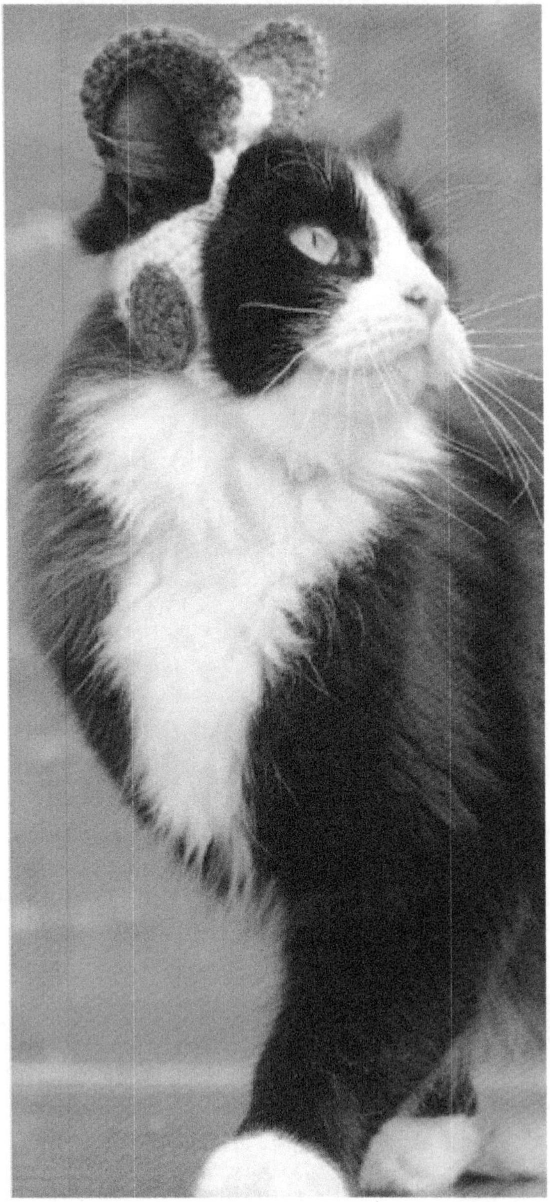

ANNA NICOLE GIVES JAWS A RUN FOR HIS MONEY IN HER SHARK ATTACK HAT.

METHOD: CROCHET

SKILL LEVEL: INTERMEDIATE

Back to Hat Selector

SIZE

TO FIT AN AVERAGE ADULT CAT

- EAR OPENING: 2 IN. (5 CM)
- WIDTH OF HAT BETWEEN EARS: 2 IN. (5 CM)

✳✳✳✳✳

SUPPLIES

- 18 YD (16 M) MEDIUM WEIGHT YARN IN A (BLUE)
- 3 YD (2.7 M) MEDIUM WEIGHT YARN IN B (RED)
- 5 YD (4.5 M) MEDIUM WEIGHT YARN IN C (WHITE)
- SIZE H8 (5 MM) CROCHET HOOK
- SIZE G6 (4 MM) CROCHET HOOK
- YARN NEEDLE

LITTLE FISH, BEWARE! SHOWCASE YOUR CAT'S PREDATOR SIDE IN THIS SHARKY HAT!

SHARK ATTACK

BASE
Using yarn A and size H8 (5 mm) hook, work 2ch, leaving a 25 in. (64 cm) tail.
Row 1: 3sc in 2nd ch, 1ch.
Row 2: 3sc, 1ch.
Row 3: 2sc in first st, 1sc, 2sc in last st, 1ch. (5sc)
Row 4: 5sc, 1ch.
Row 5: 2sc in first st, 3sc, 2sc in last st, 1ch. (7sc)
Row 6: 7sc, 1ch.
Row 7: 2sc in first st, 5sc, 2sc in last st, 1ch. (9sc)
Row 8: 9sc, 1ch.
Row 9: 2sc in first st, 7sc, 2sc in last st, 1ch. (11sc)
Row 10: 11sc, 1ch.
Row 11: 2sc in first st, 9sc, 2sc in last st, 1ch. (13sc)
FIRST EAR HOLE
Row 12: 1sc, 11ch, 1sc in last st, 1ch.
MIDDLE SECTION
Rows 13–22: 13sc, 1ch.
SECOND EAR HOLE
Row 23: 1sc, 11ch, 1sc in last st, 1ch.
Row 24: 13sc, 1ch.
Row 25: 1sc, skip next st, 9sc, skip next st, 1sc, 1ch. (11sc)
Row 26: 11sc, 1ch.
Row 27: 1sc, skip next st, 7sc, skip next st, 1sc, 1ch. (9sc)
Row 28: 9sc, 1ch.
Row 29: 1sc, skip next st, 5sc, skip next st, 1sc, 1ch. (7sc)
Row 30: 7sc, 1ch.

Row 31: 1sc, skip next st, 3sc, skip next st, 1sc, 1ch. (5sc)
Row 32: 5sc, 1ch.
Row 33: 1sc, skip next st, 1sc, skip next st, 1sc, 1ch. (3sc)
Row 34: 3sc, 1ch.
Row 35: 1sc in last st.

To create ties, work 25ch, snip yarn, and pull through loop tightly. Trim tail. Work 25ch at beg of base, using 25 in. (64 cm) tail.

FIN
Using yarn A and size G6 (4 mm) hook, work 12ch.
Row 1: Skip first ch, 11sc, 1ch.

Row 2: Skip first st, 9sc, 1ch.
Row 3: 7sc, skip next st, 1sc in last st, 1ch. (8sc)
Row 4: 7sc, 1ch. (7sc)
Row 5: 1sc, skip next st, 3sc, skip next st, 1sc, 1ch. (5sc)
Row 6: 1sc, skip next st, 1sc, skip next st, 1sc, 1ch. (3sc)
Row 7: Skip first st, 2sc, 1ch.
Row 8: 2sc, 1ch.
Row 9: Skip first st, 1sc, 1ch.
Row 10: 1sc.

Cut yarn, leaving a 8 in. (20 cm) tail. Weave the tail from the first row through to the last row of the fin. Stitch to the center of the middle section of the hat base, running needle through the bottom edge of the fin. The fin will be straighter on one side—that's the side that should face the front. Use the pictures for reference if necessary. You may need to reinforce your stitches, as you want the fin to stand upright.

FIN: 2½ X 2 IN. (6 X 5 CM) HIGH

TEETH EDGE

Using yarn B and size G6 (4 mm) hook, work 34 sl sts evenly along front edge of the hat base. Cut yarn, pull through loop securely, and weave in both ends to the underside of the hat. Next, using yarn C and size G6 (4 mm) hook, work 4ch through the first red sl st. Slip st in the same sp, 1sc in next red sl st, [4ch and slip st in same sp, 1sc] rep to end of row. Cut yarn, pull through loop securely, and weave in both ends to the underside of the hat.

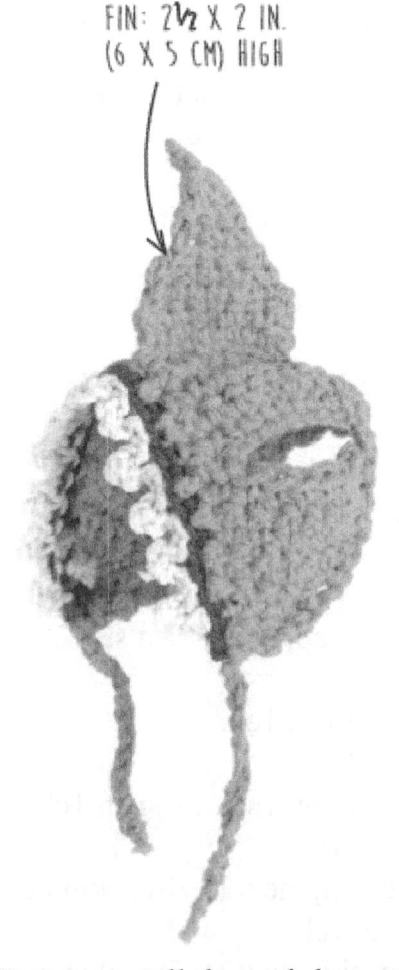

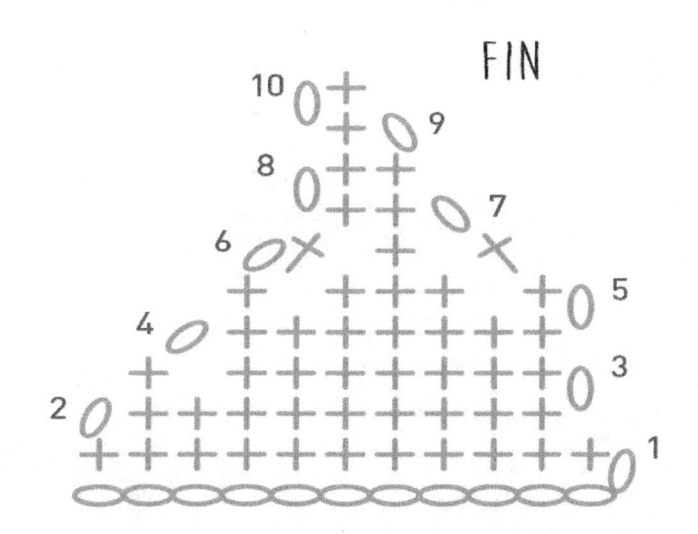

FIN

BASE

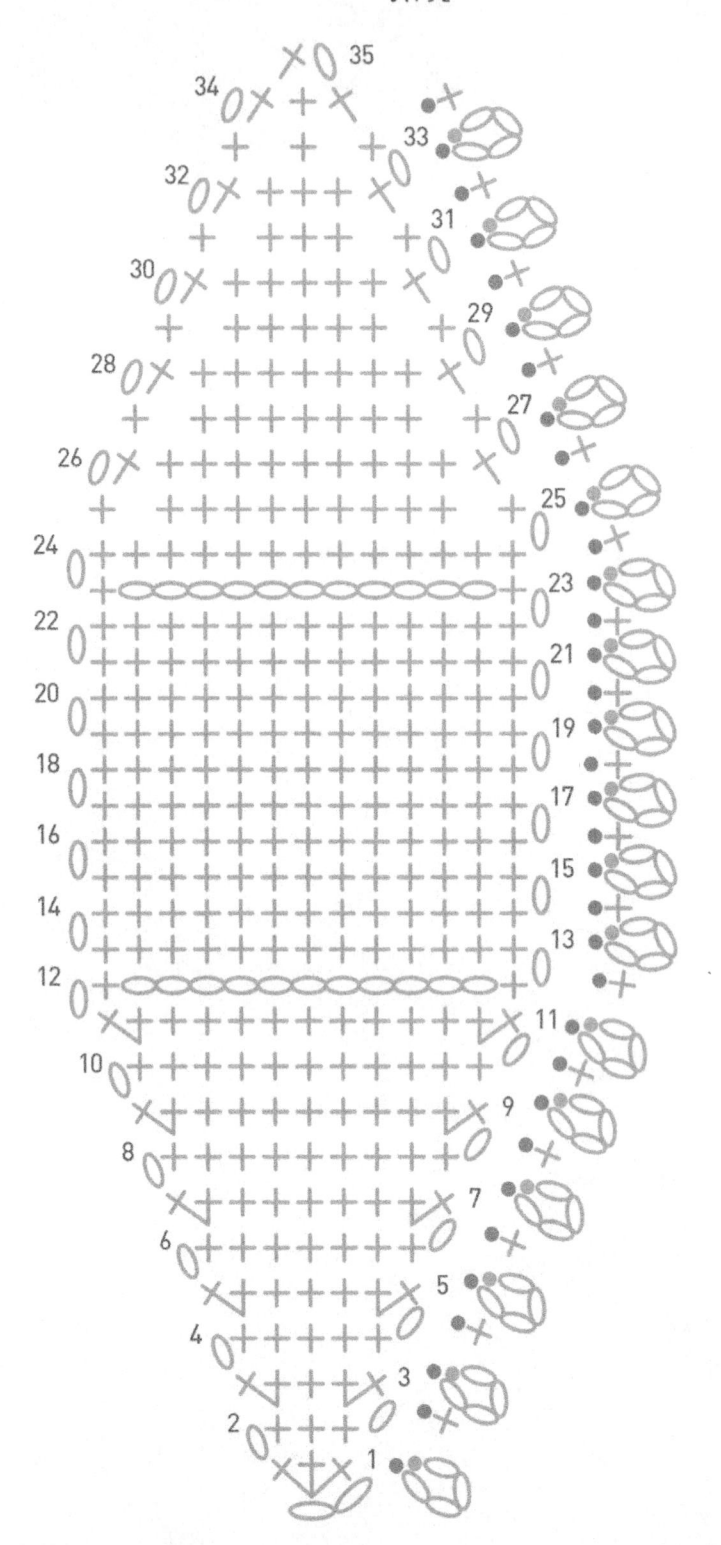

○ ch
• sl st
+ sc

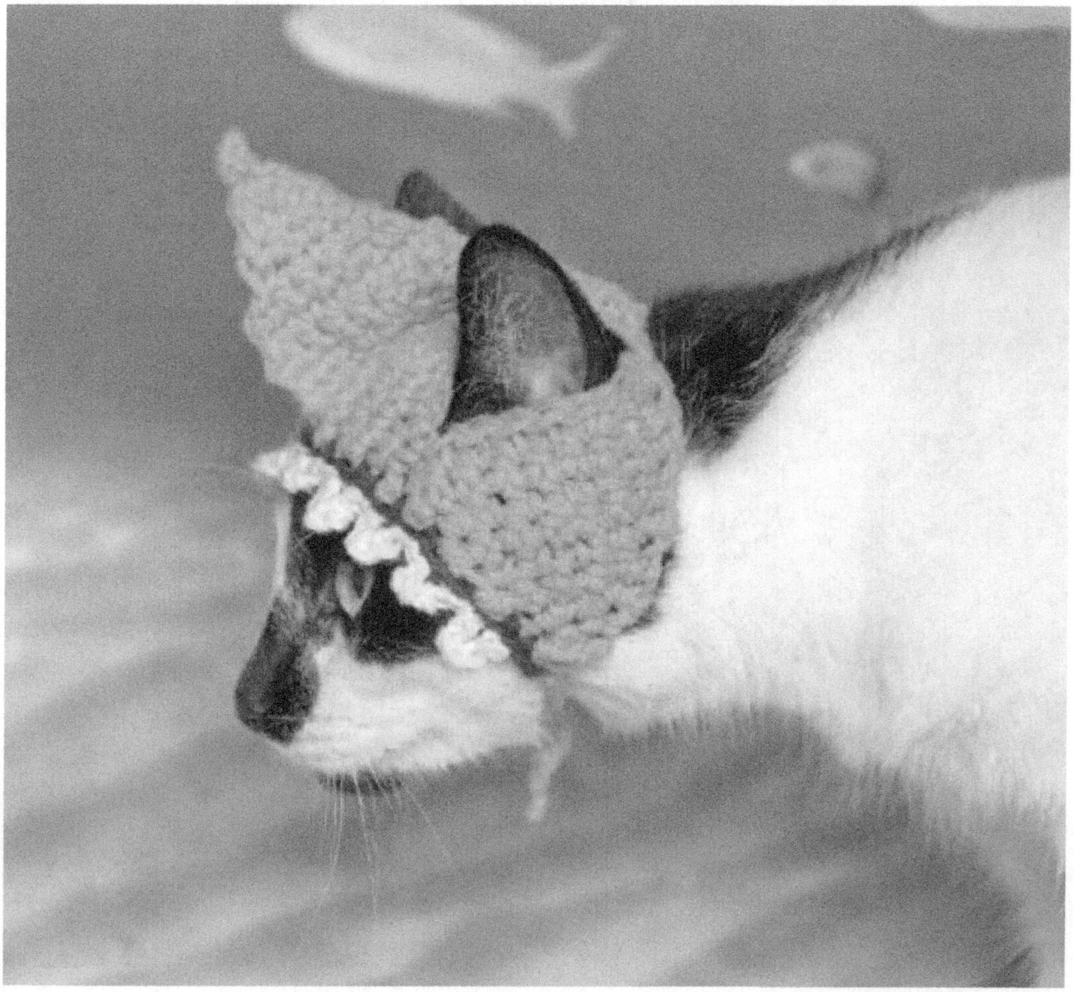

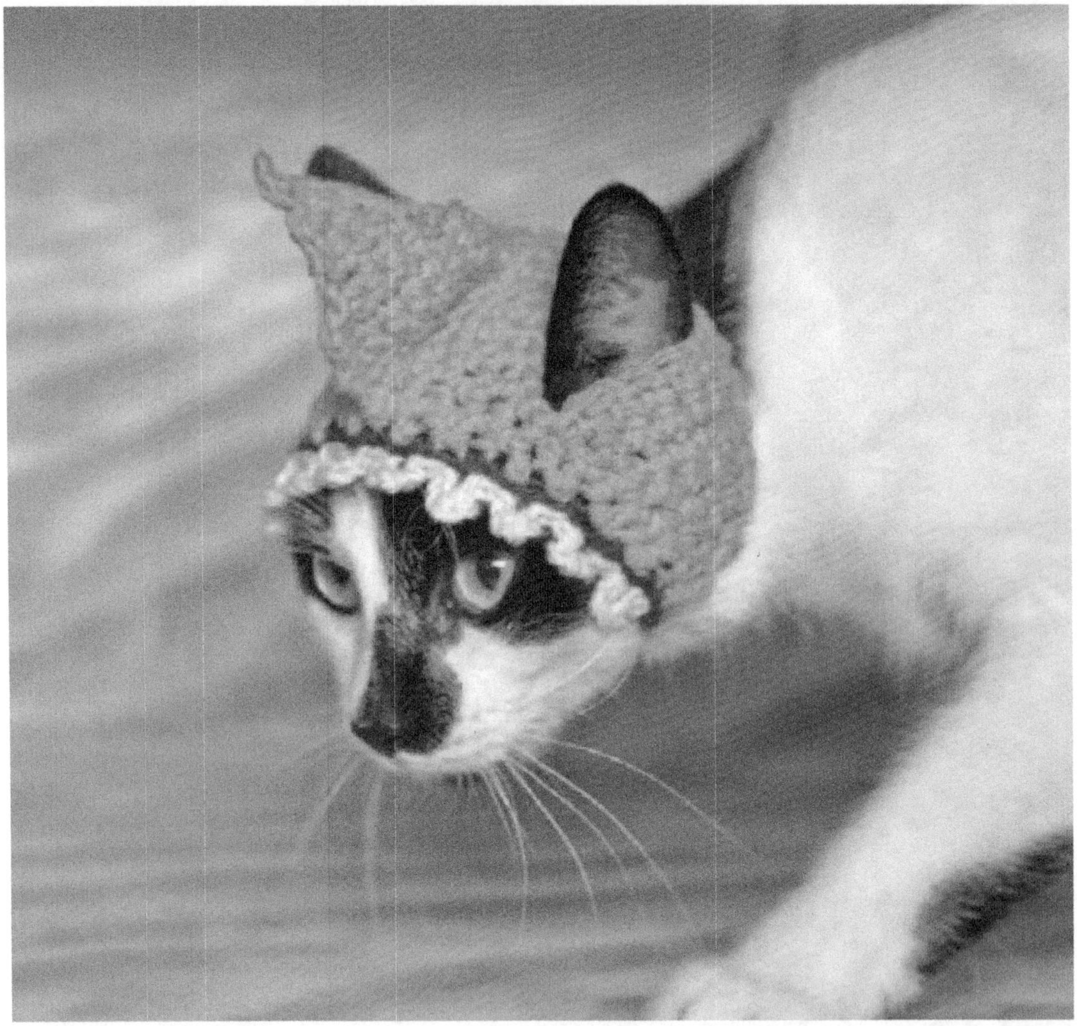

METHOD: CROCHET

SKILL LEVEL: DIFFICULT

Back to Hat Selector

SIZE

TO FIT AN AVERAGE ADULT CAT
- EAR OPENING: 2 IN. (5 CM)
- WIDTH OF HAT BETWEEN EARS: 2½ IN. (6 CM)

✳✳✳✳✳

SUPPLIES
- 30 YD (27 M) WORSTED WEIGHT YARN IN A (RED)
- 10 YD (9 M) WORSTED WEIGHT YARN IN B (WHITE)
- SIZE G6 (4 MM) CROCHET HOOK
- YARN NEEDLE
- POLYESTER FIBERFILL
- POM POM MAKER (OPTIONAL)

PADDING AROUND ON THE ROOFTOPS, WHO DOES KITTY DISCOVER? GOOD OLD SANTA CLAUS!

SANTA PAWS

BASE
Using yarn A, work 2ch, leaving a 25 in. (64 cm) tail.
Row 1: 3sc in 2nd ch, 1ch.
Row 2: 3sc, 1ch.
Row 3: 2sc in first st, 1sc, 2sc in last st, 1ch. (5sc)
Row 4: 5sc, 1ch.
Row 5: 2sc in first st, 3sc, 2sc in last st, 1ch. (7sc)
Row 6: 7sc, 1ch.
Row 7: 2sc in first st, 5sc, 2sc in last st, 1ch. (9sc)
Row 8: 9sc, 1ch.
Row 9: 2sc in first st, 7sc, 2sc in last st, 1ch. (11sc)
Row 10: 11sc, 1ch.
Row 11: 2sc in first st, 9sc, 2sc in last st, 1ch. (13sc)
FIRST EAR HOLE
Row 12: 1sc, 11ch, 1sc in last st, 1ch.
MIDDLE SECTION
Rows 13–22: 13sc, 1ch.
SECOND EAR HOLE
Row 23: 1sc, 11ch, 1sc in last st, 1ch.
Row 24: 13sc, 1ch.
Row 25: 1sc, skip next st, 9sc, skip next st, 1sc, 1ch. (11sc)
Row 26: 11sc, 1ch.
Row 27: 1sc, skip next st, 7sc, skip next st, 1sc, 1ch. (9sc)
Row 28: 9sc, 1ch.

POPPY IS FULL OF FESTIVE CHEER IN HER SANTA HAT.

Row 29: 1sc, skip next st, 5sc, skip next st, 1sc, 1ch. (7sc)
Row 30: 7sc, 1ch.
Row 31: 1sc, skip next st, 3sc, skip next st, 1sc, 1ch. (5sc)
Row 32: 5sc, 1ch.
Row 33: 1sc, skip next st, 1sc, skip next st, 1sc, 1ch. (3sc)
Row 34: 3sc, 1ch.
Row 35: 1sc in last st.
Work 25ch, snip yarn, and pull through loop tightly. Trim tail. Work 25ch at beg of base, using 25 in. (64 cm) tail.

HAT

Do not join at end of rounds. If necessary, place a marker to show start of round.
Using yarn A, work 2ch.
Rnd 1: 4sc in 2nd ch.
Rnd 2: 1sc in each st around. (4sc)
Rnd 3: 2sc in each st around. (8sc)
Rnds 4–5: 1sc in each st around.
Rnd 6: [1sc, 2sc in next st] 4 times. (12sc)
Rnds 7–9: 1sc in each st around.
Rnd 10: [1sc, 2sc in next st] 6 times. (18sc)
Rnds 11–13: 1sc in each st around.
Rnd 14: [1sc, 2sc in next st] 9 times. (27sc)
Rnds 15–17: 1sc in each st around.
Rnd 18: [2sc, 2sc in next st] 9 times. (36sc)
Rnd 19: [8sc, 2sc in next st] 4 times. (40sc)
Rnds 20–21: 1sc in each st around.

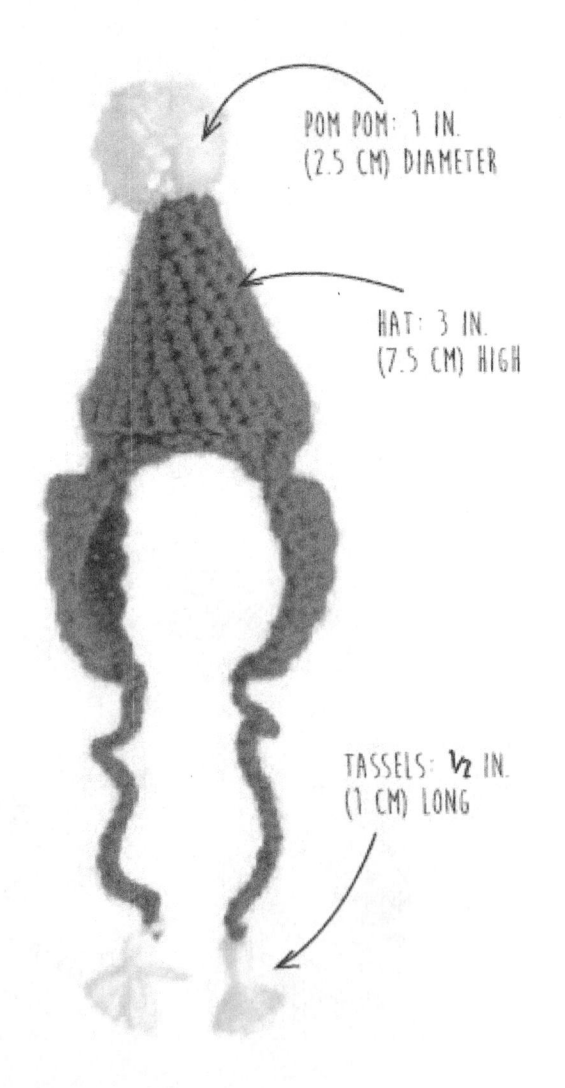

Snip yarn, leaving a 20 in. (51 cm) tail, and pull through loop tightly. Use this tail to attach the hat to the base.

ASSEMBLY

Using yarn B, make a 1 in. (2.5 cm) pom pom and two ½ in. (1 cm) tassels. Attach pom pom securely to top of hat. Attach one tassel on end of each tie. Lightly stuff hat top with polyester fiberfill, being careful to evenly distribute filling. Stitch onto center of the base of hat with 20 in. (51 cm) tail.

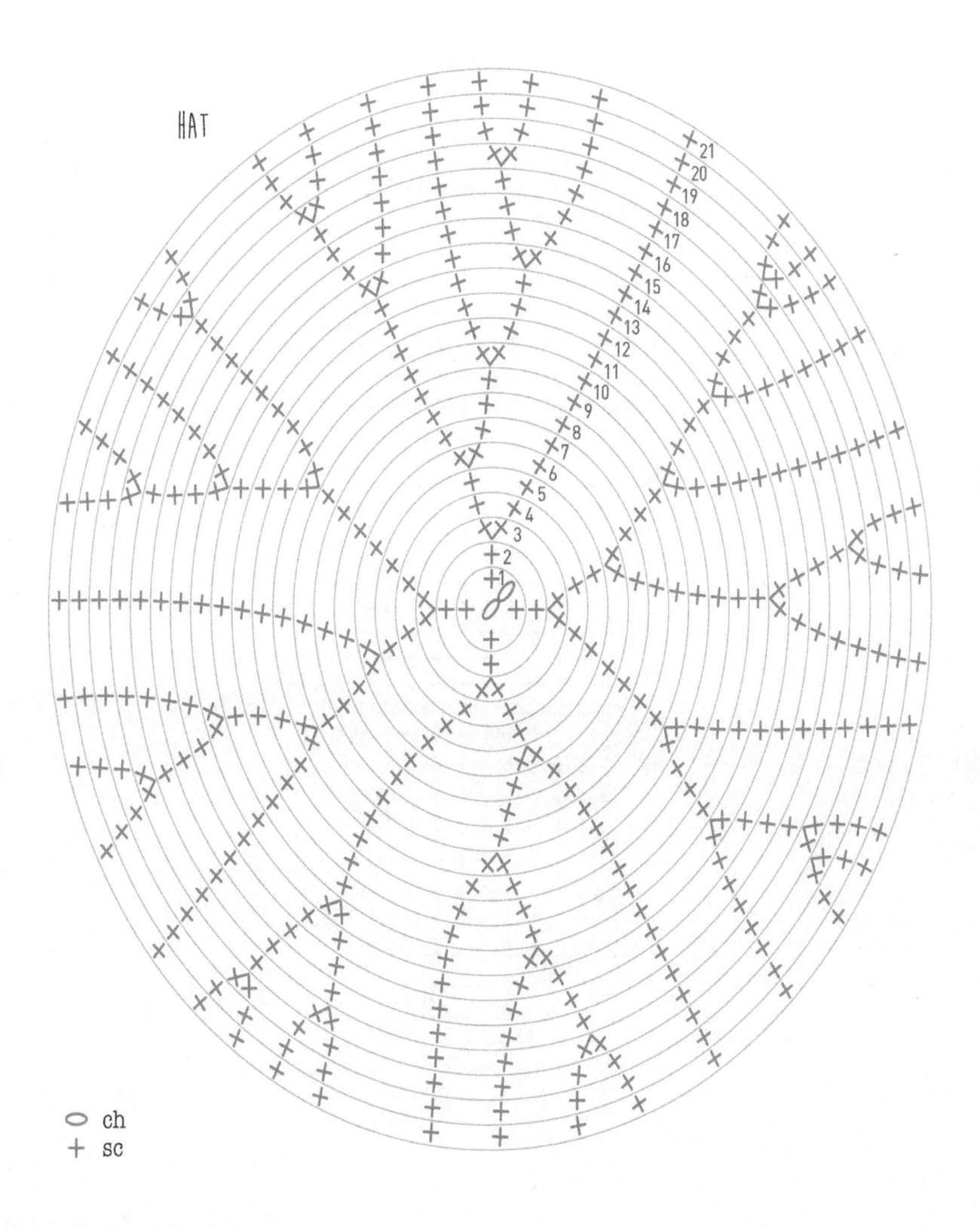

HAT

+ 21
+ 20
+ 19
+ 18
+ 17
+ 16
+ 15
+ 14
+ 13
+ 12
+ 11
+ 10
+ 9
+ 8
+ 7
+ 6
+ 5
+ 4
+ 3
+ 2
+ 1

○ ch
+ sc

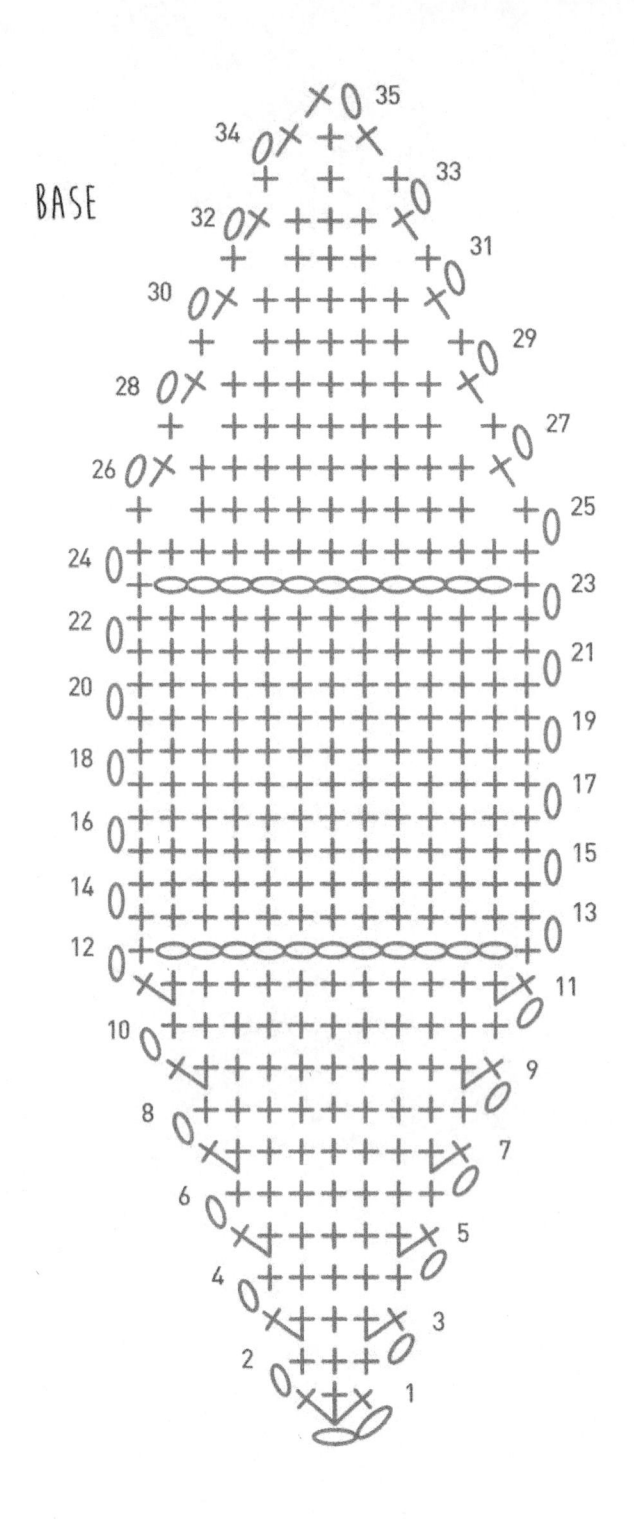

BASE

METHOD: CROCHET

SKILL LEVEL: DIFFICULT

Back to Hat Selector

SIZE

TO FIT AN AVERAGE ADULT CAT
- EAR OPENING: 2½ IN. (6 CM)
- WIDTH OF HAT BETWEEN EARS: 2½ IN. (6 CM)

✳✳✳✳✳

SUPPLIES

- 30 YD (27 M) WORSTED WEIGHT YARN IN A (YELLOW)
- 10 YD (9 M) WORSTED WEIGHT YARN IN B (WHITE)
- 10 YD (9 M) WORSTED WEIGHT YARN IN C (ORANGE)
- SIZE G6 (4 MM) CROCHET HOOK
- YARN NEEDLE
- POLYESTER FIBERFILL

TRICK OR TREAT, HERE'S A HAT THAT'S EXTRA SWEET!

CANDY CORN

BASE
Using yarn A, work 2ch, leaving a 25 in. (64 cm) tail.
Row 1: 3sc in 2nd ch, 1ch.
Row 2: 3sc, 1ch.
Row 3: 2sc in first st, 1sc, 2sc in last st, 1ch. (5sc)
Row 4: 5sc, 1ch.
Row 5: 2sc in first st, 3sc, 2sc in last st, 1ch. (7sc)
Row 6: 7sc, 1ch.
Row 7: 2sc in first st, 5sc, 2sc in last st, 1ch. (9sc)
Row 8: 9sc, 1ch.
Row 9: 2sc in first st, 7sc, 2sc in last st, 1ch. (11sc)
Row 10: 11sc, 1ch.
Row 11: 2sc in first st, 9sc, 2sc in last st, 1ch. (13sc)
FIRST EAR HOLE
Row 12: 1sc, 11ch, 1sc in last st, 1ch.
MIDDLE SECTION
Rows 13–22: 13sc, 1ch.
SECOND EAR HOLE
Row 23: 1sc, 11ch, 1sc in last st, 1ch.
Row 24: 13sc, 1ch.
Row 25: 1sc, skip next st, 9sc, skip next st, 1sc, 1ch. (11sc)
Row 26: 11sc, 1ch.
Row 27: 1sc, skip next st, 7sc, skip next st, 1sc, 1ch. (9sc)
Row 28: 9sc, 1ch.
Row 29: 1sc, skip next st, 5sc, skip next st, 1sc, 1ch. (7sc)
Row 30: 7sc, 1ch.
Row 31: 1sc, skip next st, 3sc, skip next st, 1sc, 1ch. (5sc)
Row 32: 5sc, 1ch.
Row 33: 1sc, skip next st, 1sc, skip next st, 1sc, 1ch. (3sc)
Row 34: 3sc, 1ch.
Row 35: 1sc in last st.

HAT: 4 IN. (10 CM) HIGH

To create ties, work 25ch, snip yarn, and pull through loop tightly. Trim tail. Work 25ch at beg of base, using 25 in. (64 cm) tail.

CANDY CORN
Using yarn B, make a magic ring.
Rnd 1: 1ch, 6sc in ring.
Rnd 2: 6sc.
Rnd 3: [2sc in next st, 2sc] twice. (8sc)
Rnds 4–5: Sc around.
Rnd 6: [2sc in next st, 3sc] twice. (10sc)
Rnds 7–8: Sc around.
Rnd 9: [2sc in next st, 4sc] twice. (12sc)

Change to yarn C.
Rnds 10–11: Sc around.
Rnd 12: [2sc in next st, 5sc] twice. (14sc)
Rnds 13–14: Sc around.
Rnd 15: [2sc in next st, 6sc] twice. (16sc)
Rnds 16–17: Sc around.
Rnd 18: [2sc in next st, 7sc] twice. (18sc)

Cut yarn, leaving a 15 in. (38 cm) tail, and pull through loop. Turn hat inside out. Sew yarn B tail to close up top gap. Weave ends to inside and finish.

ASSEMBLY
Lightly and evenly stuff candy corn with polyester fiberfill. Be careful to maintain a soft square point at the top of the candy corn. Stitch hat onto the center of the base with yarn C tail, with the square top facing toward the front (not the ears) of the hat. Use the photos if necessary for reference. Secure ends to underside of base and finish.

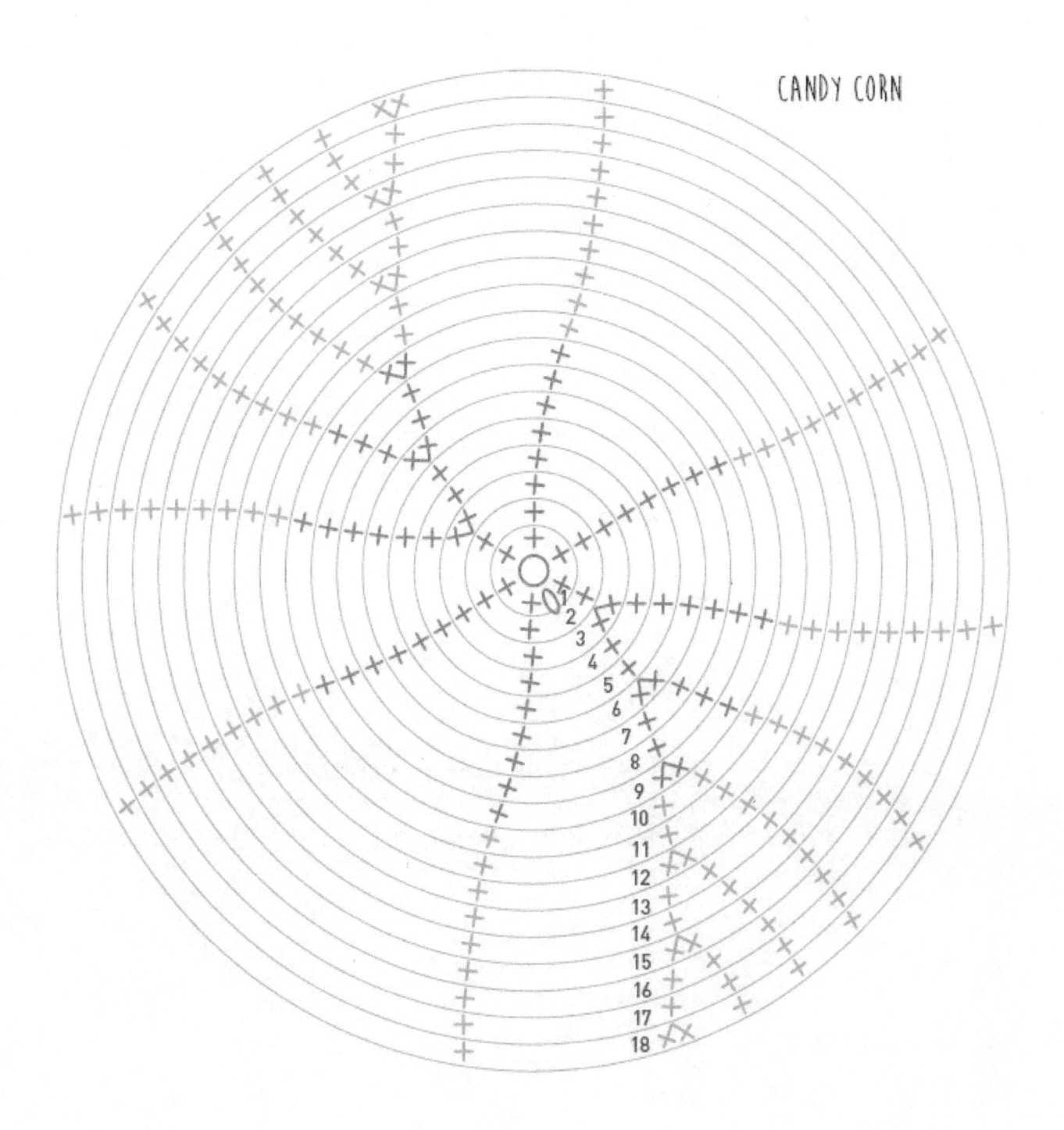

CANDY CORN

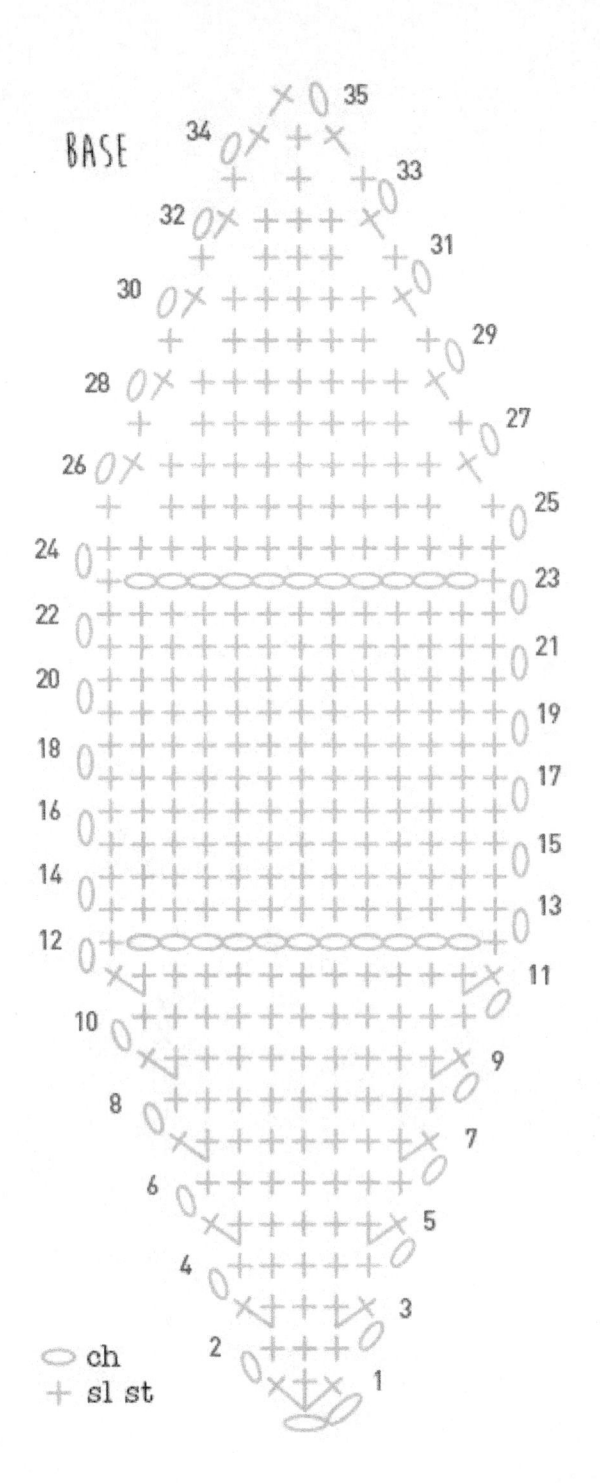

BASE

○ ch
+ sl st

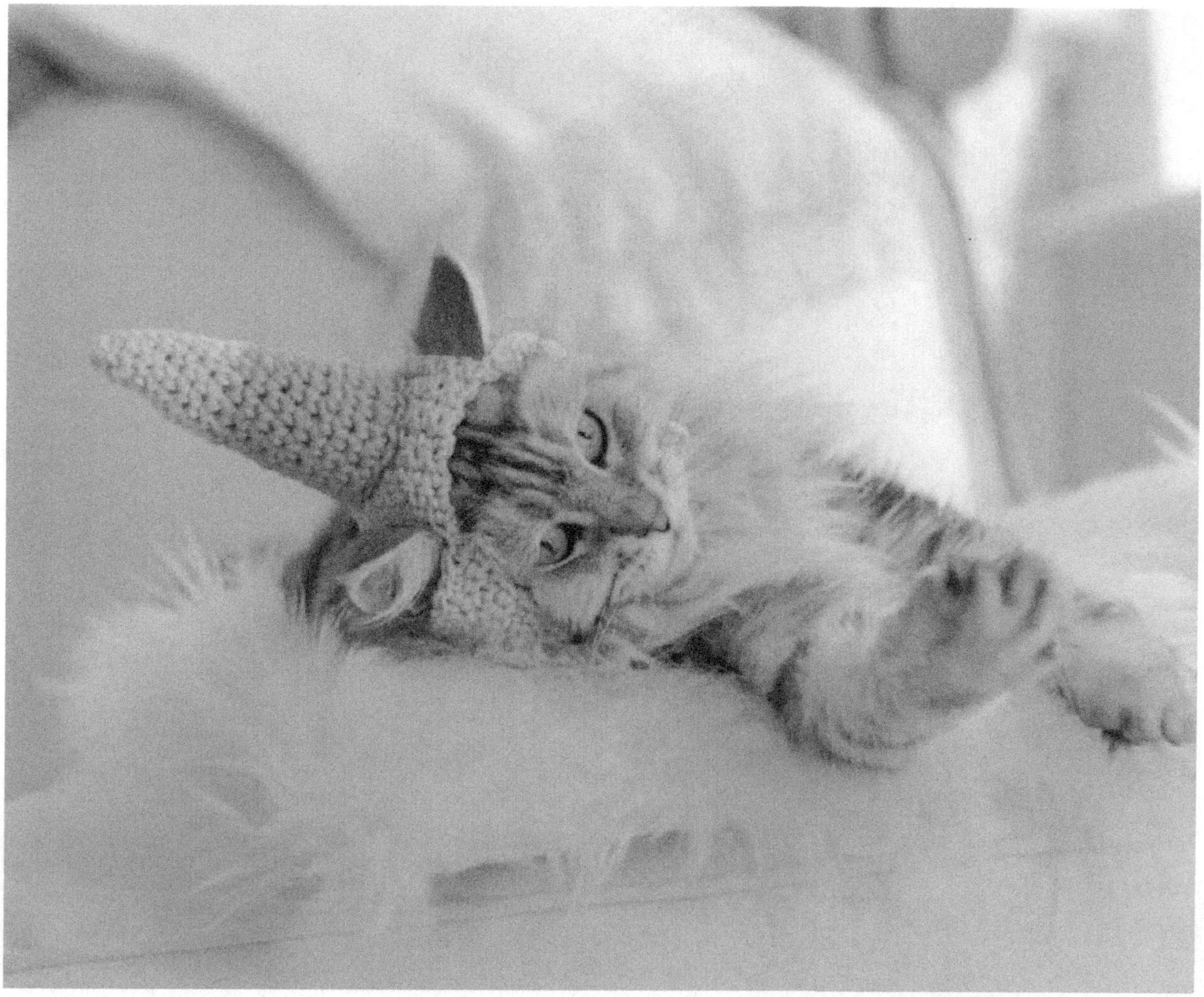

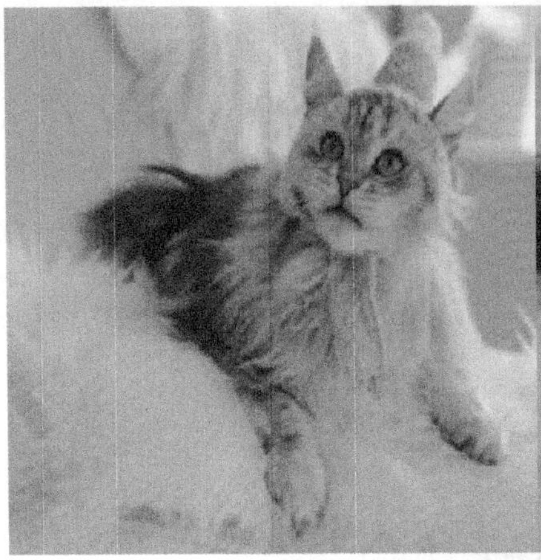

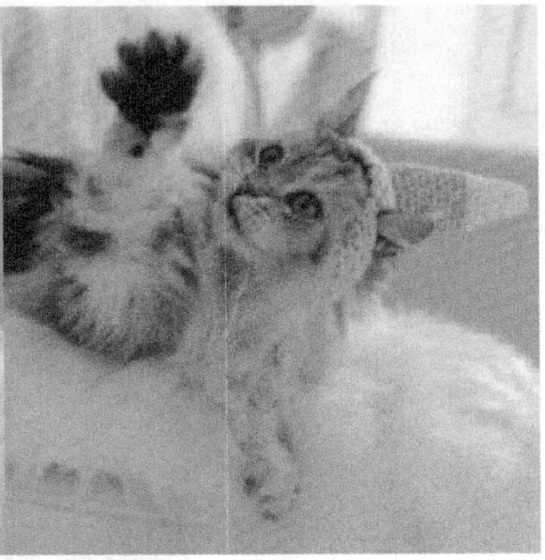

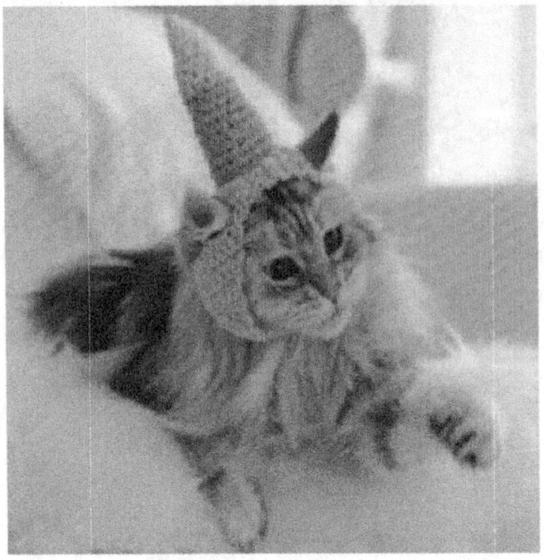

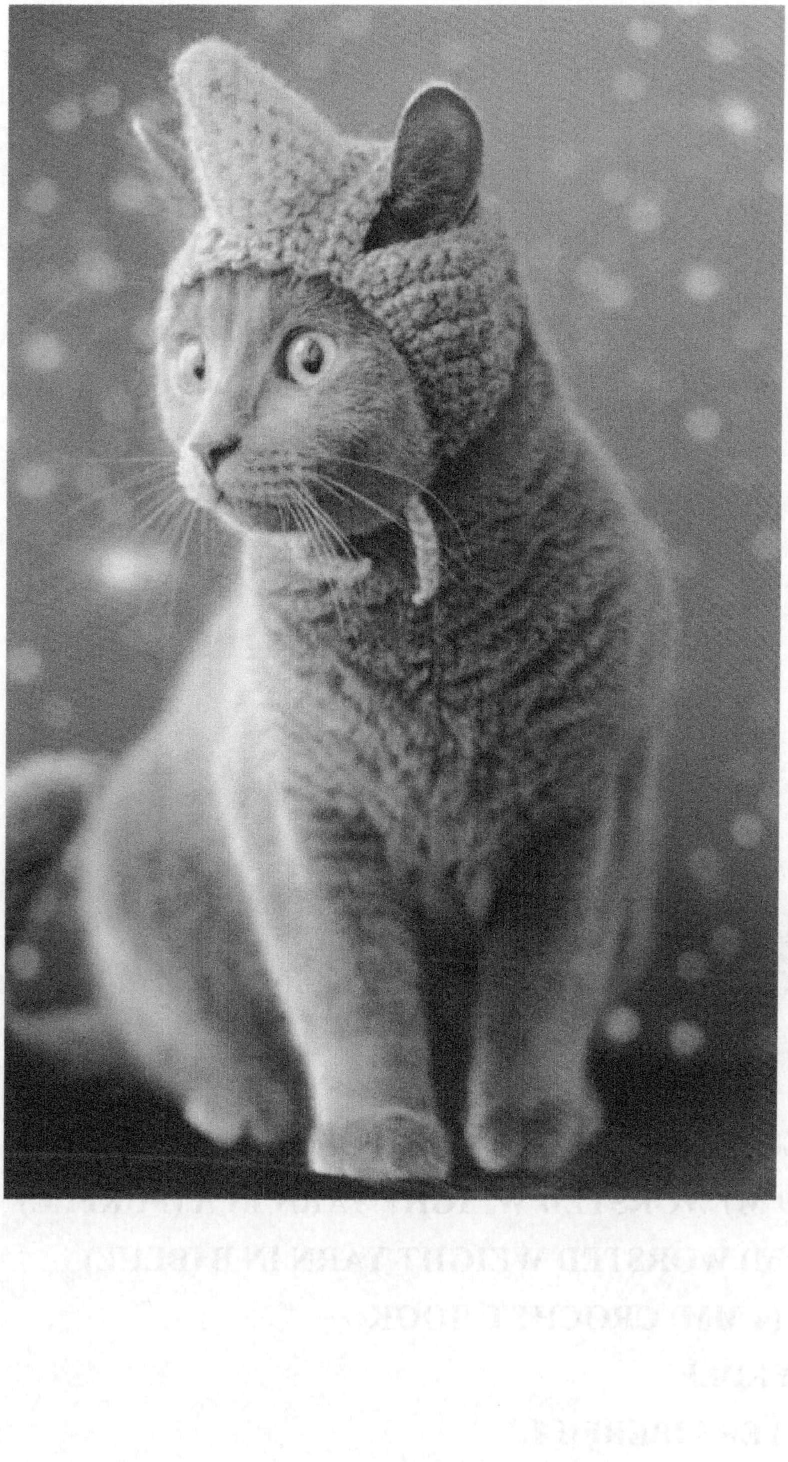

METHOD: CROCHET

SKILL LEVEL: DIFFICULT

Back to Hat Selector

SIZE

TO FIT AN AVERAGE ADULT CAT
- EAR OPENING: 2 IN. (5 CM)
- WIDTH OF HAT BETWEEN EARS: 2½ IN. (6 CM)

✺✺✺✺✺

SUPPLIES

- 21 YD (19 M) WORSTED WEIGHT YARN IN A (PURPLE)
- 10 YD (9 M) WORSTED WEIGHT YARN IN B (BLUE)
- SIZE G6 (4 MM) CROCHET HOOK
- YARN NEEDLE
- POLYESTER FIBERFILL

ONCE EXTINCT, THE RARE UNICORN CAT GRACES ONLY THE MOST FANTASTICAL OF HOMES. ADD A BRIGHTLY COLORED FRINGE MANE ALONG THE TOP OF THE HAT FOR A LITTLE FLAIR!

UNICORN

BASE
Using yarn A, work 2ch, leaving a 3 in. (7.5 cm) tail.
Row 1: 3sc in 2nd ch, 1ch.
Row 2: 3sc, 1ch.
Row 3: 2sc in first st, 1sc, 2sc in last st, 1ch. (5sc)
Row 4: 5sc, 1ch.
Row 5: 2sc in first st, 3sc, 2sc in last st, 1ch. (7sc)
Row 6: 7sc, 1ch.
Row 7: 2sc in first st, 5sc, 2sc in last st, 1ch. (9sc)
Row 8: 9sc, 1ch.
Row 9: 2sc in first st, 7sc, 2sc in last st, 1ch. (11sc)
Row 10: 11sc, 1ch.
Row 11: 2sc in first st, 9sc, 2sc in last st, 1ch. (13sc)
FIRST EAR HOLE
Row 12: 1sc, 11ch, 1sc in last st, 1ch.
MIDDLE SECTION
Rows 13–22: 13sc, 1ch.
SECOND EAR HOLE
Row 23: 1sc, 11ch, 1sc in last st, 1ch.
Row 24: 13sc, 1ch.
Row 25: 1sc, skip next st, 9sc, skip next st, 1sc, 1ch. (11sc)
Row 26: 11sc, 1ch.
Row 27: 1sc, skip next st, 7sc, skip next st, 1sc, 1ch. (9sc)

Row 28: 9sc, 1ch.
Row 29: 1sc, skip next st, 5sc, skip next st, 1sc, 1ch. (7sc)
Row 30: 7sc, 1ch.
Row 31: 1sc, skip next st, 3sc, skip next st, 1sc, 1ch. (5sc)
Row 32: 5sc, 1ch.
Row 33: 1sc, skip next st, 1sc, skip next st, 1sc, 1ch. (3sc)
Row 34: 3sc, 1ch.
Row 35: 1sc in last st.
Cut yarn, leaving a 3 in. (7.5 cm) tail. Weave in both tails to underside of base.

UNICORN HORN
(Make 1)
Using yarn B, make a magic ring.
Rnd 1: 1ch, 4sc in ring.
Rnd 2: Sc in each st around, sl st in first sc. (4sc)
Rnd 3: [2sc in next st, 1sc] twice. (6sc)
Rnd 4: Sc around.
Rnd 5: [2sc in next st, 2sc] twice. (8sc)
Rnd 6: Sc around.
Rnd 7: [2sc in next st, 3sc] twice. (10sc)
Rnd 8: Sc around.
Rnd 9: [2sc in next st, 4sc] twice. (12sc)
Rnd 10: Sc around.
Rnd 11: [2sc in next st, 5sc] twice. (14sc)
Rnd 12: Sc around.
Cut yarn, leaving a 15 in. (38 cm) tail, and pull through loop tightly.

ASSEMBLY
Weave in tail from top of unicorn horn, making sure to close any gaps. Lightly stuff horn with polyester fiberfill, making sure to stuff evenly. Using 15 in. (38 cm) tail, securely stitch horn to the center of the base, close to front of hat.

Using yarn B, measure out two pieces of yarn 25 in. (64 cm) each. To create ties at each end of the base, use one piece of yarn and pull a loop through the end of the hat, work 25ch, pull yarn through loop tightly, and snip. Repeat with other piece on the other side of the hat.

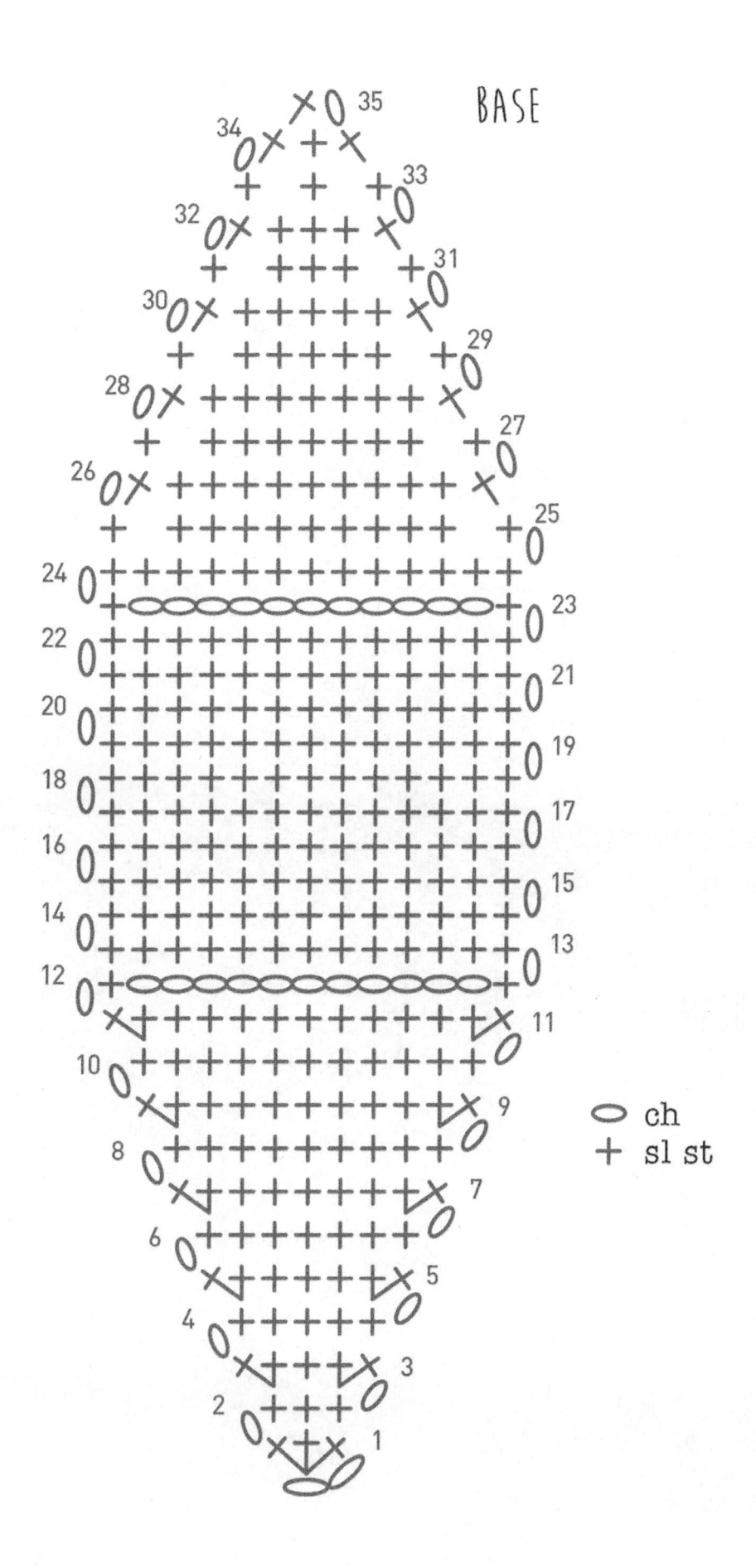

BASE

○ ch
+ sl st

HORN

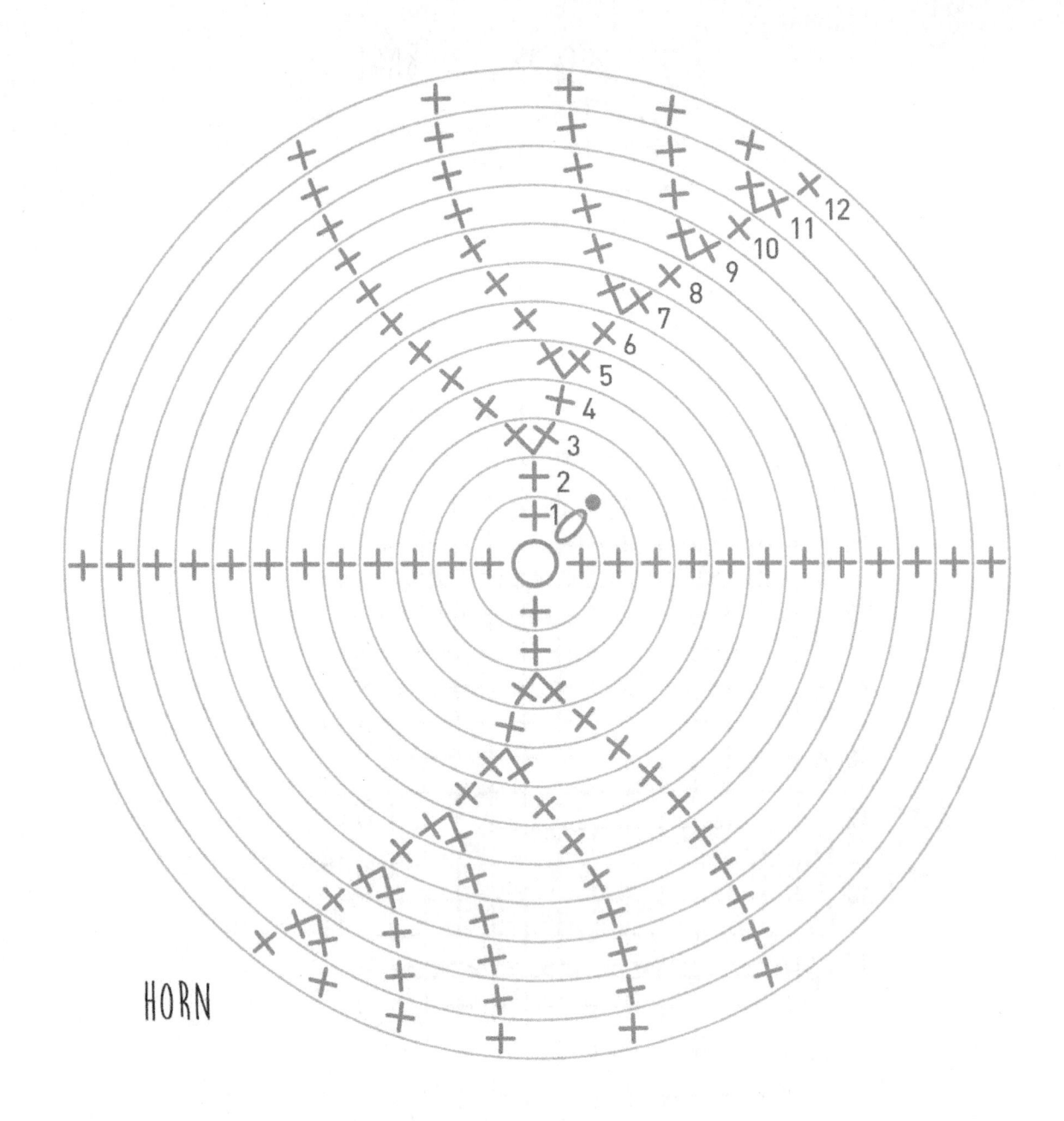

GUS LOOKS ENCHANTING IN HIS UNICORN HAT.

METHOD: CROCHET

SKILL LEVEL: DIFFICULT

Back to Hat Selector

SIZE
TO FIT AN AVERAGE ADULT CAT
- LENGTH: 5 IN. (13 CM)
- WIDTH: 3 IN. (7.5 CM)

✳✳✳✳✳

SUPPLIES
- 40 YD (37 M) WORSTED WEIGHT YARN IN A (BEIGE)
- 6 YD (5.5 M) WORSTED WEIGHT YARN IN B (BLUE)
- 6 YD (5.5 M) WORSTED WEIGHT YARN IN C (ORANGE)
- SIZE E4 (3.5 MM) CROCHET HOOK
- YARN NEEDLE

TRANSPORT YOUR CAT TO THE WILD WEST IN THIS PERFECTLY BROKEN-IN COWBOY HAT!

COWBOY HAT

HAT
Do not turn work in this pattern.
Using yarn A, work 6ch.

Rnd 1: 2sc in 2nd ch, 1sc in next 3ch, 3sc in next ch. Continuing along other side of chain, work 1sc in back loop of next 4ch, sl st to beg ch, 1ch. (12 sts)

Rnd 2: 1sc in first st, 2sc in next st, 4sc, [2sc in next st] twice, 4sc, sl st to beg ch, 1ch. (15sts)

Rnd 3: 2sc in next 2sts, 5sc, 2sc in next 2 sts, sl st to next sc; this marks new position for start of rnd. (This will cause the hat to start to curl, which is part of the shaping.)

For the following rnds, use a marker at the beg of each rnd to help keep your place. From Rnds 4–13 inclusive, work 1ch at beg of each rnd and end each rnd with sl st to beg ch.

Rnd 4: [5sc, 2sc in next st] 4 times.
Rnd 5: [6sc, 2sc in next st] 4 times.
Rnd 6: [7sc, 2sc in next st] 4 times.
Rnd 7: [8sc, 2sc in next st] 4 times.
Rnd 8: [9sc, 2sc in next st] 4 times.
Rnd 9: [10sc, 2sc in next st] 4 times.
Rnds 10–12: Sc around.

BRIM
Rnd 13: 2sc in each st around, sl st to beg ch.
Rnd 14: Sl st in each st around.
Snip yarn, leaving enough tail to weave in ends.

TO SHAPE
You have created two points at the top of your hat. These points should face the ears, and you should use the starting tail to stitch into place a dip in between these points. You may find it helpful to turn to the WS, or inside, of the hat and, pinching between the points, secure this shape with a few stitches.

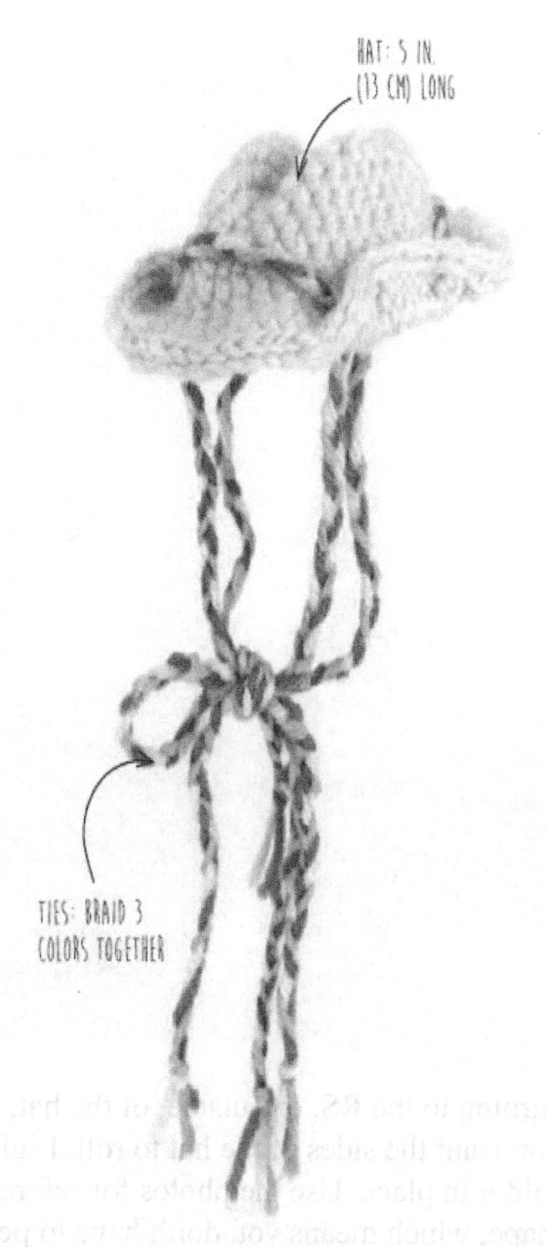

Turning to the RS, or outside, of the hat, you will need to stitch your brim into place. You want the sides of the hat to roll. Lightly roll each side, and work 3 or 4 stitches to hold it in place. Use the photos for reference. Properly broken in hats have an authentic shape, which means you don't have to perfectly stitch the brim rolls. Just remember that the front and back need to be flat. Stitching the brim is what gives the hat its final shape, so adjust it according to your liking. An experienced crocheter could give this hat a stiffer shape by stuffing it. You would need to crochet an oval, or small base, to stitch your hat onto and to hold the stuffing in. You could use the other patterns in this book as a reference for this if you wish.

TIES
(Make 2)

Using a strand of all three yarn colors, make two braided ties that each measure 1 yd (90 cm). You could also use a ¼ in. (0.5 cm) wide ribbon or trim of your choice for ties.

To attach ties to the hat, take one tie and pull it through the front left side (near the rolled brim) of the hat. Use a larger crochet hook if necessary. Now pull the other end of the tie through the front right side of the hat (again near the rolled brim). Repeat with other tie at the back of the hat. Use the photos for reference if necessary.

TO WEAR

You now have 4 ties hanging underneath your hat, two on the right and two on the left. Carefully tie the two left and the two right ties together, in a bow under the chin. Make sure the ties are on either side of the ear on each side. This ensures a more comfortable fit (your cat's ears should be clear of the hat). If you need the hat to be a bit smaller, or larger, on top, adjust the roll of the brim.

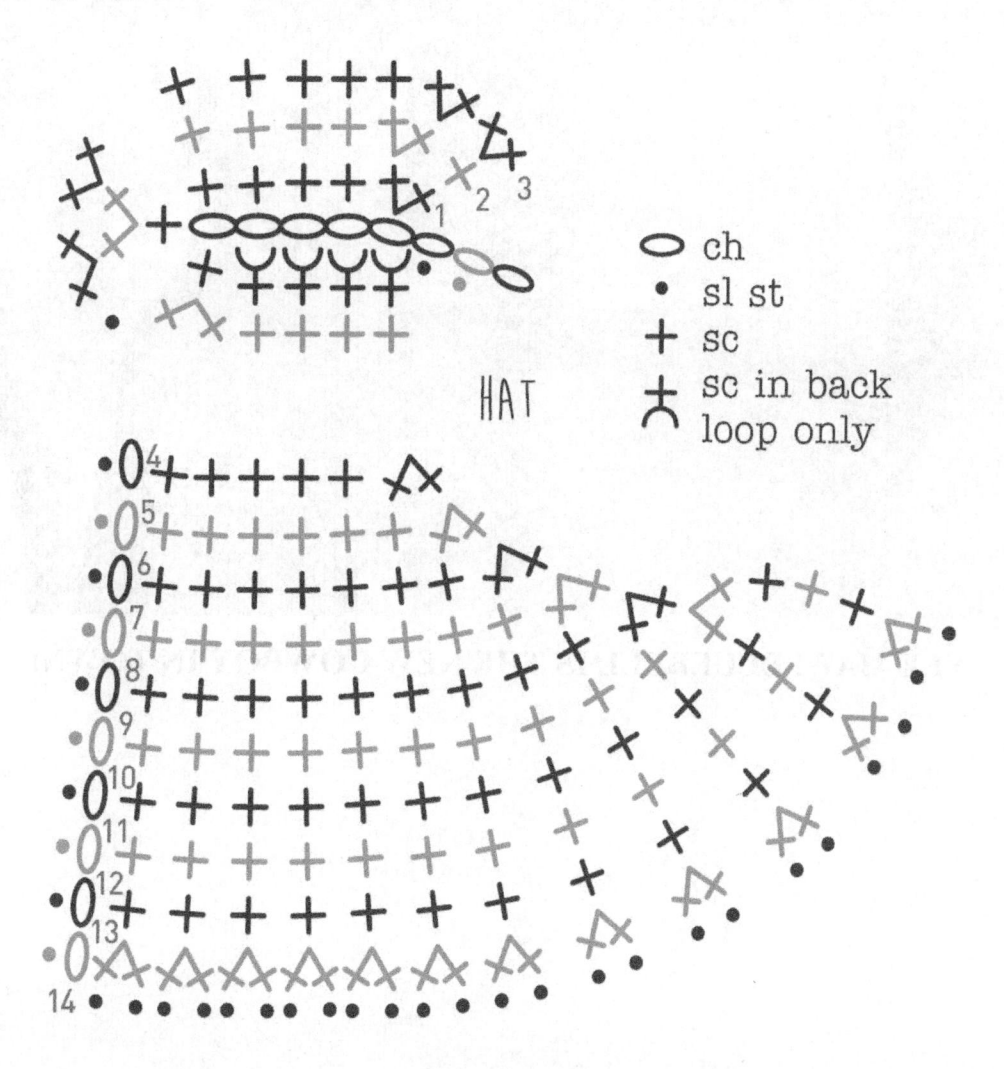

YEE-HAW! BLUEBELL IS THE NEW COWBOY IN TOWN!

Eyelash yarn

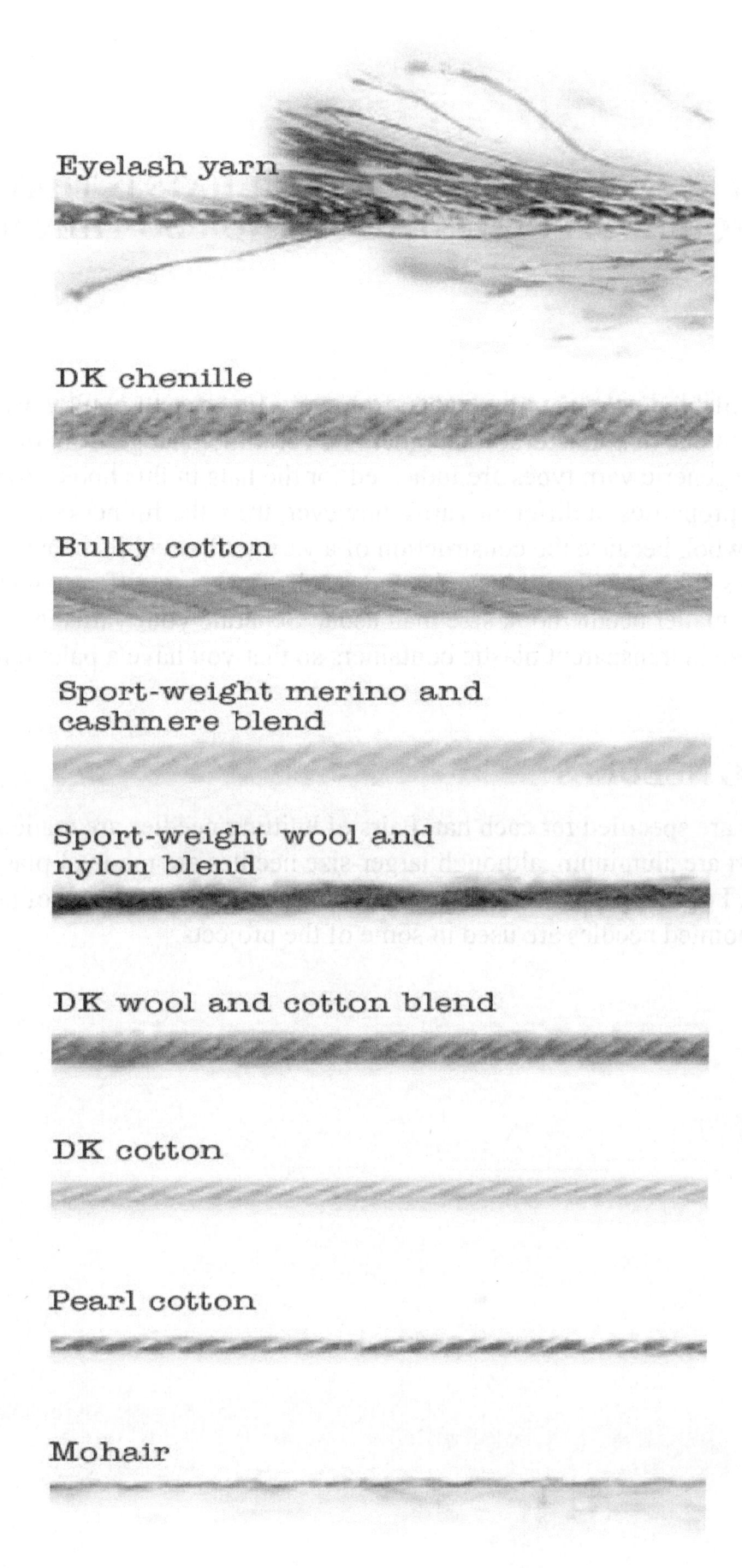

DK chenille

Bulky cotton

Sport-weight merino and cashmere blend

Sport-weight wool and nylon blend

DK wool and cotton blend

DK cotton

Pearl cotton

Mohair

MATERIALS AND EQUIPMENT

THE NEAT THING ABOUT MAKING CAT HATS IS THAT THEY DON'T REQUIRE SPECIALIST TOOLS, NOR DO THEY USE MUCH YARN.

YARNS

Yarns are available in a range of weights, from very fine to extra bulky. Because yarns may vary from one manufacturer to another and certainly change from one fiber to another, only generic yarn types are indicated for the hats in this book. You should be aware of the properties of different yarns, however, from the fullness of cotton to the elasticity of wool, because the construction of a yarn will affect its behavior and characteristics, and so will influence the end result. Try using different gauges and, if in doubt, use a smaller needle/hook size than usual. Separate your yarns into color groups and keep these in transparent plastic containers so that you have a palette of colors to work with.

KNITTING NEEDLES

Needle sizes are specified for each hat. Pairs of knitting needles are made in a variety of lengths. Most are aluminum, although larger-size needles are made of plastic to reduce their weight. For most of the designs in this book, a conventional pair of needles is used, but double-pointed needles are used in some of the projects.

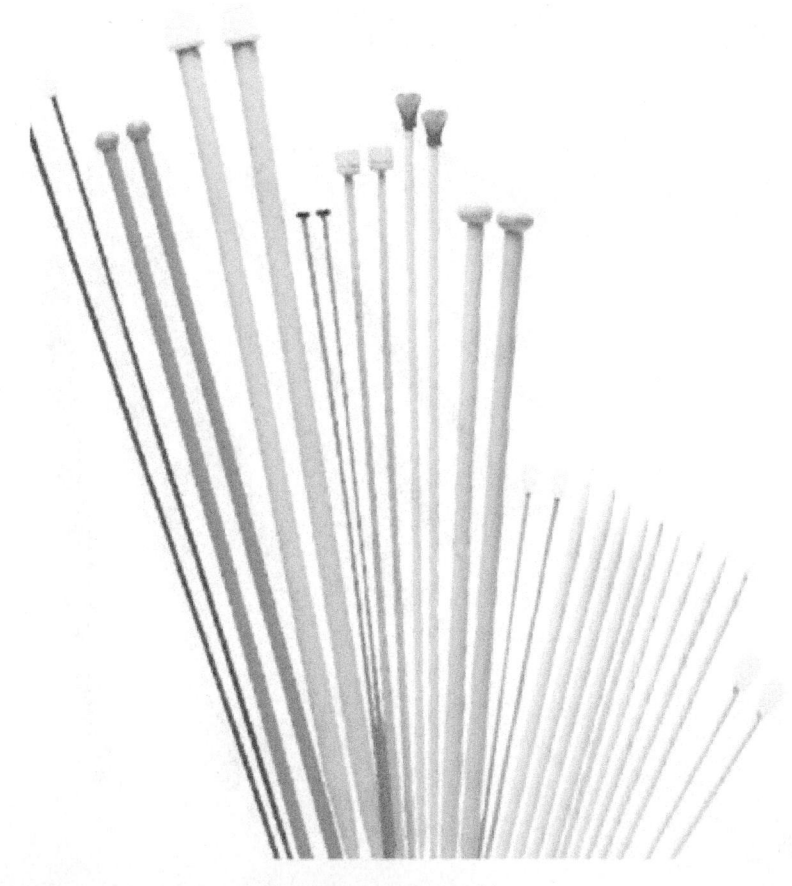

Knitting needles are available in a variety of sizes and materials.

CROCHET HOOKS

Crochet hooks are available in a wide range of sizes and materials. Most hooks are made from aluminum or plastic. Small sizes of steel hooks are made for working with very fine yarns. Handmade wooden, bamboo, and horn hooks are also available.

Hook sizes are quoted differently in the United States and Europe, and some brands of hook are labeled with more than one numbering system. Choosing a hook is largely a matter of personal preference. The design of the hook affects the ease of working considerably. Look for a hook that has a comfortable grip.

Assorted crochet hooks.

Row counters are useful.

STUFFING MATERIALS AND ADDITIONAL EQUIPMENT

POLYESTER FIBERFILL

There are a number of options open to you when it comes to stuffing your hat, including foam, cotton batting, and polyester fiberfill. I recommend polyester fiberfill, a synthetic fiber that is extremely lightweight and also washable. It has a soft feel and it bounces back into shape. It tends to clump less than many of the other stuffing materials. It is also widely available.

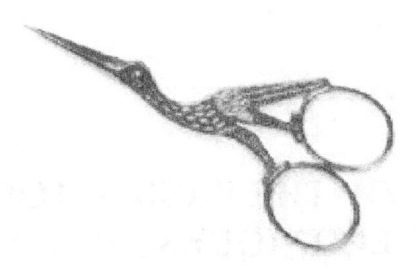

Always have a sharp pair of scissors handy.

TAPE MEASURE

Essential for measuring lengths of yarn, choose one that features both inches and centimeters on the same side.

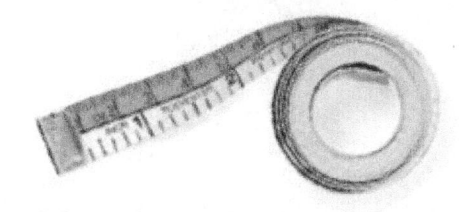

A tape measure lets you check that you have adequate yarn.

MARKERS AND ROW COUNTERS

Ready-made markers can be used to indicate a repeat or to help count stitches in a chain. Similarly, a row counter may help you to keep track of the number of rows you have worked, but in knitting this is usually easy if you remember to include the stitches on the needle as a row.

KNITTING TECHNIQUES

HERE IS A REMINDER OF THE BASICS, TOGETHER WITH A FEW SUGGESTSIONS AND TECHNIQUES THAT MIGHT BE NEW TO A BEGINNING KNITTER.

SLIPKNOT

1 Putting a slipknot on the needle makes the first stitch of the cast on. Loop the yarn around two fingers of the left hand, the ball end on top. Dip the needle into the loop, catch the ball end of the yarn, and pull it through the loop.

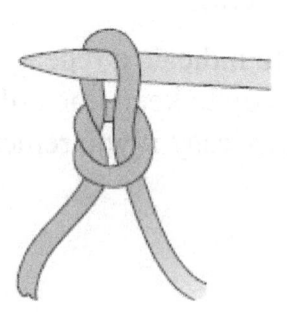

2 Pull the ends of the yarn to tighten the knot. Tighten the ball end to bring the knot up to the needle.

CASTING ON

There are several cast on methods, each with its own merits.

Thumb method
Sometimes called long-tail cast on, this uses a single needle and produces an elastic edge.

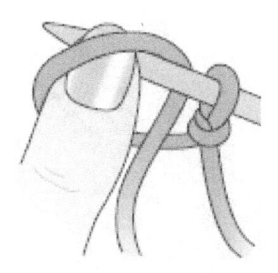

1 Leaving an end about three times the length of the required cast on, put a slipknot on the needle. Holding the yarn end in the left hand, take the left thumb under the yarn and upward. Insert the needle in the loop made on the thumb.

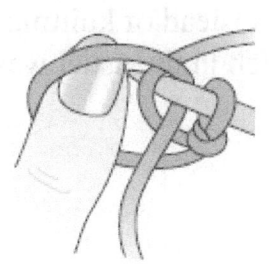

2 Use the ball end of the yarn to make a knit stitch, slipping the loop off the thumb. Pull the yarn end to close the stitch up to the needle. Continue making stitches in this way. The result looks like a row of garter stitch because the yarn has been knitted off the thumb.

Cable cast on
This two-needle method gives a firm edge with the appearance of a rope.

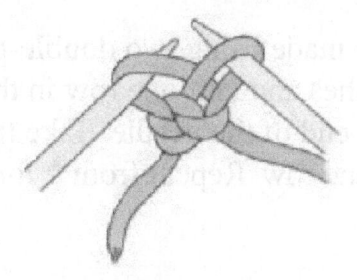

1 Put a slipknot on one needle. Use the other needle and the ball end of the yarn to knit into the loop on the left-hand needle without slipping it off. Transfer the new stitch to the left-hand needle.

2 Insert the right-hand needle between the new stitch and the next stitch, and then make another stitch as before. Continue making stitches in this way.

Knitted cast on
Make a cable cast on as above, but instead of knitting between stitches, insert the right-hand needle in the front of each stitch in the usual way. This gives a softer edge than the cable method.

I-CORD

A very useful round cord can be made using two double-pointed needles. Cast on four (or the required number of) stitches and knit one row in the usual way. *Without turning, slide the stitches to the opposite end of the needle. Take the yarn firmly across the wrong side from left to right and knit one row. Repeat from * for the required length.

BINDING AND FASTENING OFF

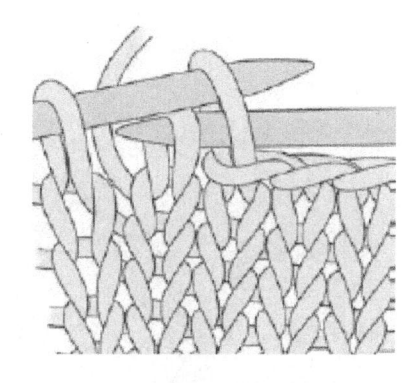

A simple knit stitch bind off is used in this book. Knit two stitches. *With the left needle, lift the first stitch over the second and off the right needle. Knit the next stitch. Repeat from * until one stitch remains. Break off the yarn, pass the end through this stitch, and tighten.

PICK UP AND KNIT

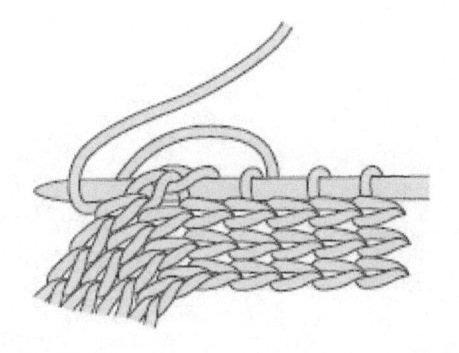

The pick up and knit technique involves knitting up new stitches along the edge of a knitted piece, ready to work in another direction. This avoids having to cast on a separate piece and join it with a seam. With RS facing you, insert the right needle under an edge stitch, take the yarn around the needle, and pull a loop through to make a stitch. Repeat for the number of stitches required, spacing the picked up stitches evenly along the edge. The next row will be a WS row.

KNITTING IN THE ROUND

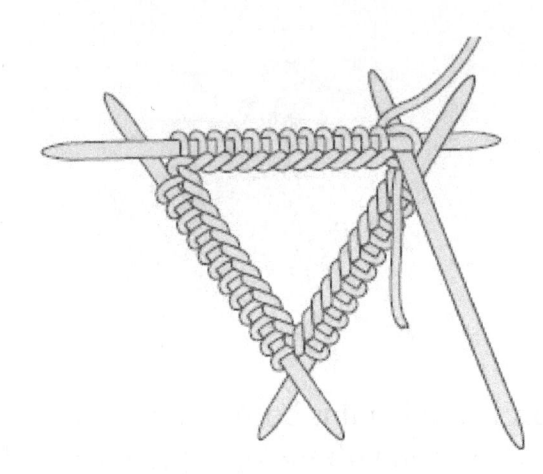

When knitting in the round using four double-pointed needles (dpns), the stitches are distributed among three of the needles and the spare needle is used to knit with. Bring the first and third needles together to form a circle and use the spare needle to work the stitches off the first (left) needle and onto the spare (right) needle in the usual way. This is done with the RS (outside) of the work facing you, unless stated otherwise. Take the yarn firmly from one double-pointed needle to the next or a ladder will appear.

CROCHET TECHNIQUES

HERE ARE A FEW REMINDERS OF THE BASICS AND SOME SUGGESTIONS FOR BUILDING ON THEM.

SLIPKNOT

1 Putting a slipknot on the hook makes the first loop of the chain that will hold the stitches of the first row or round. Loop the yarn around two fingers of the left hand, the ball end to the front. Insert the hook in the loop, catch the ball end of the yarn, and pull it through the loop.

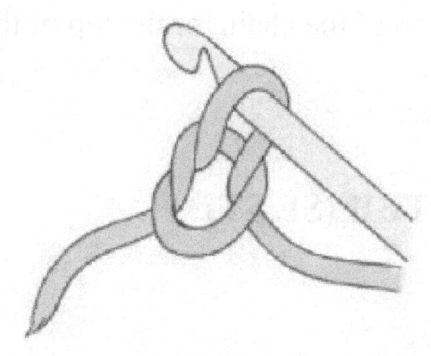

2 Pull the ends of yarn to tighten the knot. Now tighten the ball end to bring the knot up to the hook.

HOOKING ACTION

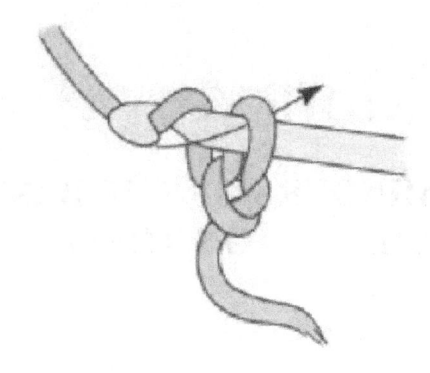

Hold the slipknot (and later the chain) between the thumb and forefinger of the left hand. Take the yarn over the second finger of the left hand so it is held taut. Take it around the little finger as well if necessary. The right hand is then free to manipulate the hook. With a turn of the wrist, guide the tip of the hook under the yarn. Catch the yarn and pull it through the loop on the hook to make a chain.

Hooking and catching is referred to as yarn over hook (abbreviation: yo). It is the action used in making a chain, a slip stitch, and, in various combinations, all other crochet stitches.

Note Unless the instructions state otherwise, the hook should be inserted under the two strands of yarn that form the top of the chain, or the top of the stitch.

WORKING A SLIP STITCH (SL ST)

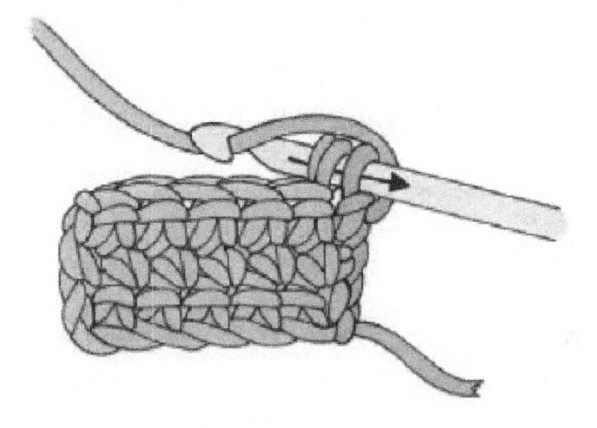

Slip stitch is the shortest of all the crochet stitches and its main uses are for joining rounds, making seams, and carrying the hook and yarn from one place to another. Insert the hook from front to back into the required stitch. Wrap the yarn over the hook (yarn over) and draw it through both the work and the loop on the hook. One loop remains on the hook and one slip stitch has been worked.

CHAIN RING

Join a number of chain stitches into a ring with a slip stitch in the first chain. Work the first round of stitches around the chain and into the center of the ring. If the yarn end is also worked around, the ring is lightly padded and this end can be pulled to tighten it.

MAGIC RING

1 To make a magic ring, first coil the yarn around two fingers and then use the hook to pull through a loop of the ball end of the yarn, as if making a slipknot (see step 1, above left). However, do not then pull the yarn tight. Holding the ring flat between the thumb and forefinger of the left hand, catch the yarn and pull it through the loop on the hook to anchor it.

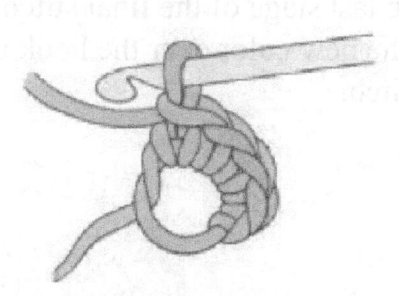

2 Working under two strands of yarn each time, make the stitches as directed and then pull the free yarn end to close the ring. Join the ring with a slip stitch in the first stitch.

JOINING IN A NEW YARN

There are several methods you can use to join in a new yarn or color.

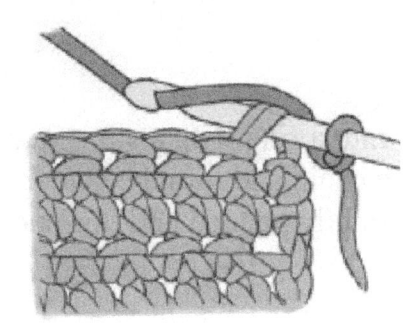

Using slip stitch
This method can be used when working any stitch. Make a slipknot in the new yarn and place it on the hook. Insert the hook into the work at the specified position and make a slip stitch with the new yarn through both stitch and slipknot. Continue working the pattern with the new yarn.

Changing colors mid-stitch
To switch neatly from an old color to a new color in the same place, you can leave the last stitch in the old color incomplete and use the new color to finish the stitch.

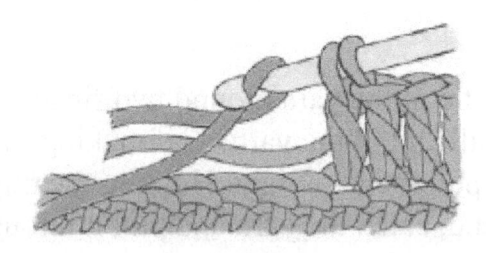

1 Using the old color, leave the last stage of the final stitch incomplete, so that there are two loops on the hook. Wrap the new color over the hook and pull it through the loops on the hook to complete the stitch.

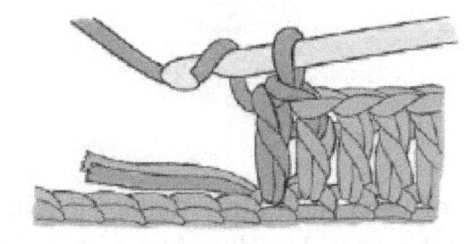

2 Continue working with the new color. You may find it easier to knot the two loose ends together before you cut the yarn no longer in use, leaving ends of about 4 in. (10 cm). Always undo the knot before weaving in the yarn ends.

ADDITIONAL TECHNIQUES

ALL THE HATS ARE EASY TO ASSEMBLE USING JUST A FEW STANDARD FINISHING TECHNIQUES. HERE ARE SOME TIPS AND SUGGESTIONS.

MARKERS

If markers are needed to count rows or repeats, use a length of contrast thread. *Lay it between stitches from front to back, make a stitch, and then bring it from back to front of the work. Repeat from * once more. It can be pulled out when it is no longer needed.

STUFFING

Use polyester fiberfill (batting) rather than cotton wool, as the latter can be rather dense and difficult to stitch through. Push the batting in firmly, one wisp at a time, using it to shape the object without distorting it. Too much batting will pack down, whereas too little will never plump up. Don't push the batting in with a pointed implement, but use something like the eraser end of a pencil. Spare matching yarn may be better than batting inside crochet, as there will be no show-through. Wind off short lengths of yarn around two fingers and push these in, one coil at a time.

ENDS

Sometimes called a tail, the end of yarn left after making the slipknot should be a reasonable length so that it can be used for sewing up. It can also be very useful for covering up imperfections, such as awkward color changes. The same applies to the end left after binding or fastening off. In these projects, ends that will not be needed for sewing up should be woven in and secured to the WS before the main assembly of the hat.

POM POMS

A couple of the hats in this book require pom poms. Either use a ready-made plastic pom pom maker or cut out two rings of cardboard.

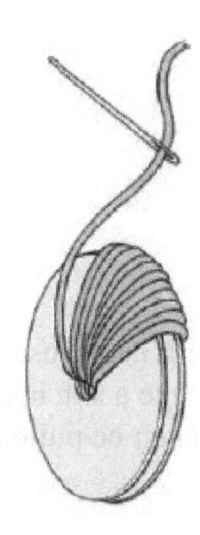

1 Place the two rings together and use a yarn needle to wrap yarn around them.

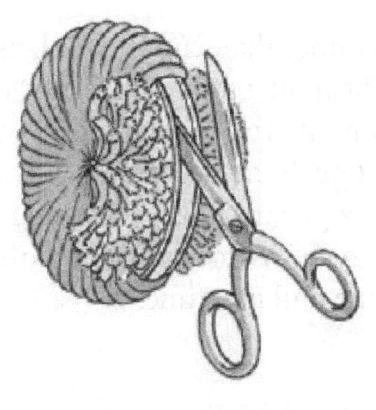

2 Starting new lengths of yarn at the outside edge, continue until the rings are tightly covered. Insert the blade of a pair of scissors between the rings and cut the yarn around the edge.

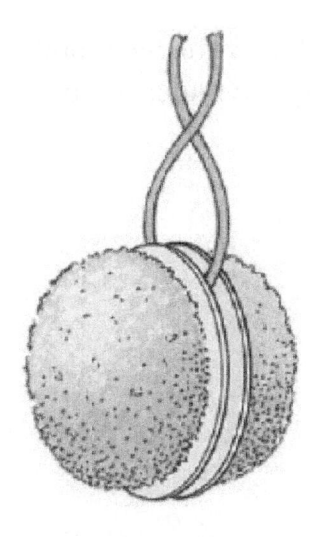

3 Tie a length of yarn around the pom pom between the rings. Knot the yarn tightly, slip the rings off, and trim the pom pom. Use the ends of yarn from the tie for attaching the pom pom to the hat.

JOINING KNITTED AND CROCHETED PIECES

It is always best to leave a lengthy tail when you cast on or bind off, as this tail can serve as your joining yarn when sewing pieces together. The projects in this book specify at which point to leave additional length. Carefully place the piece to be attached in the correct location, using sewing pins if necessary. Using a blunt yarn needle and the tail (or a length of matching yarn), stitch small upright stitches through the edge of the piece being joined to the main piece of the project. When done in the same shade of yarn, these stitches should be invisible. Once attached, pull the yarn to the wrong side of the knitted or crocheted object (usually the underside of the hat) and secure with several knots. Weave in ends.

ABBREVIATIONS

GENERAL

rep	repeat
rnd(s)	round(s)
RS	right side(s)
st(s)	stitch(es)
WS	wrong side(s)

KNITTING

dpn(s)	double pointed needle(s)
k	knit
k2tog	knit 2 together
kfb	knit in front and back of stitch to make two stitches from one
p	purl

CROCHET

beg	beginning
ch	chain
sc	single crochet
sl st	slip stitch
sp	space
yo	yarn forward and over hook to make a stitch

READING CHARTS

Each crochet design is accompanied by a chart that should be read with the written instructions.

The chart represents the right side of the work.

CHARTS IN ROWS

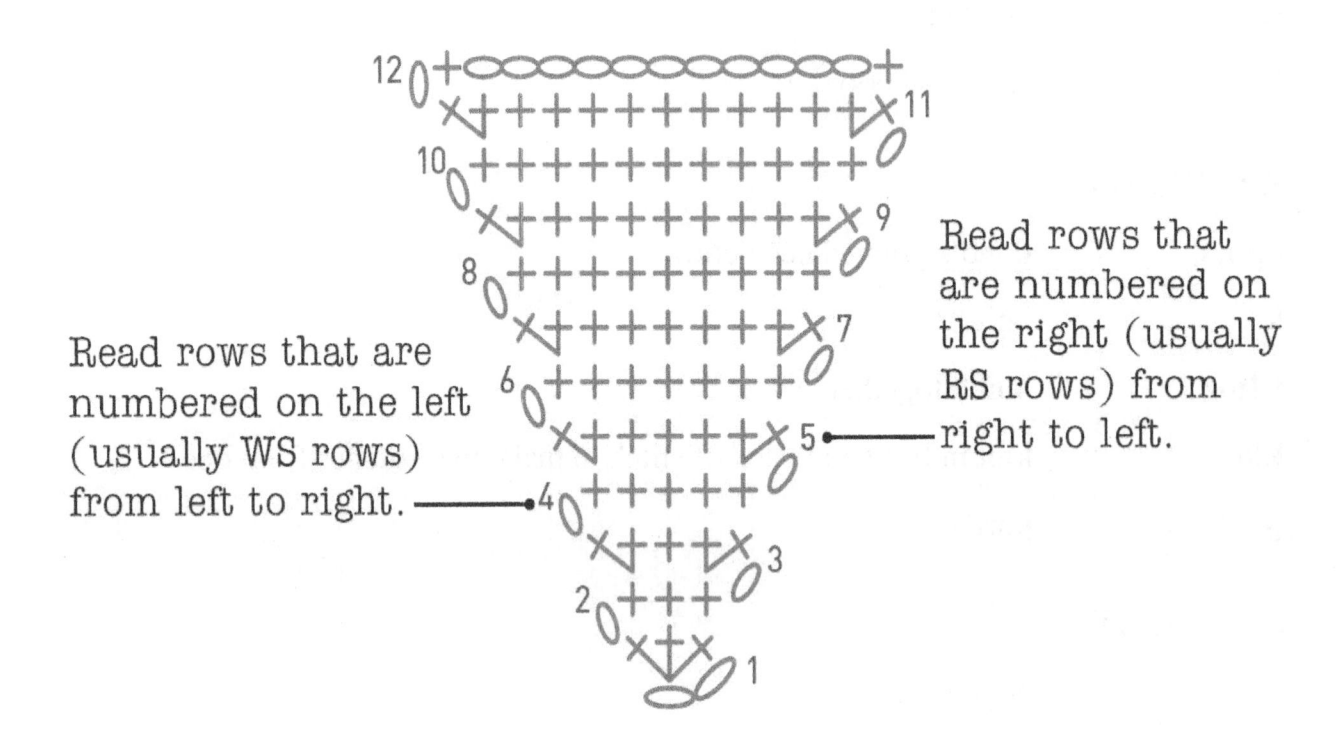

Read rows that are numbered on the left (usually WS rows) from left to right.

Read rows that are numbered on the right (usually RS rows) from right to left.

CHARTS IN ROUNDS

Charts for working in the round begin at the center and are read counterclockwise (in the same direction as working).

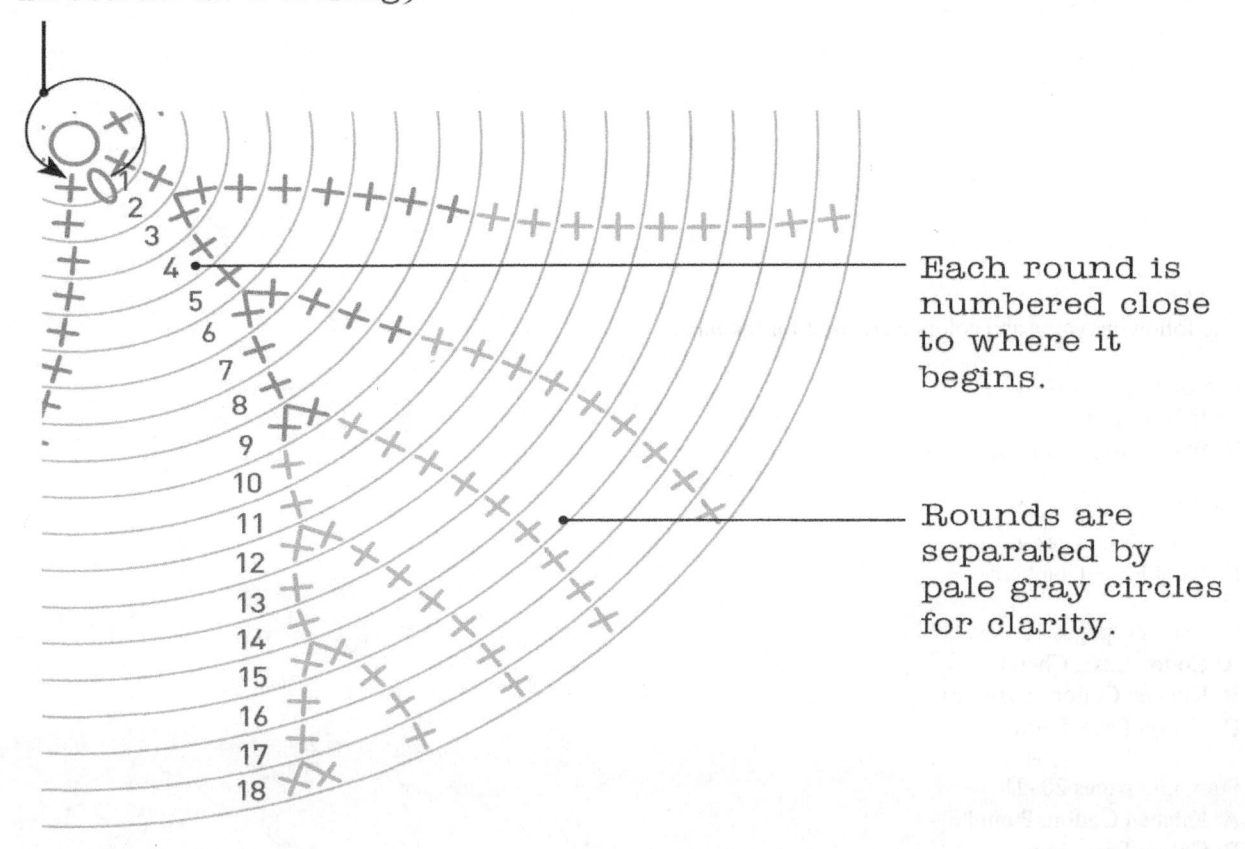

Each round is numbered close to where it begins.

Rounds are separated by pale gray circles for clarity.

YARNS USED

The following yarns and colors were used for the hats:

Dinosaur, pages 10–13
A: Jiffy, Avocado
B: Wool Ease, Pumpkin

Bobble Hat, pages 14–15
A: Wool Ease, Seaspray
B: Wool Ease, Cranberry

Strawberry, pages 16–19
A: Cotton Ease, Cherry
B: Kitchen Cotton, Snap Pea
C: Cotton Ease, Snow

Pumpkin, pages 20–21
A: Kitchen Cotton, Pumpkin
B: Cotton Ease, Lime

Sports Cap, pages 22–23
A: Wool Ease, Ranch Red
B: Vanna's Choice, White
C: Wool Ease, Sea Spray

Spring Chick, pages 24–25
A: Romance, Passion
B: Fun Yarn, Black
C: Kitchen Cotton, Pumpkin

Punk Mohawk, pages 26–29
A: Vanna's Choice, Black
B: Roving Wool, Hot Pink

Bunny, pages 30–31
Nature's Choice Organic Cotton, Almond

Turkey, pages 32–35
A: Jiffy, Caffe
B: Fun Yarn, Red
C: Fun Yarn, Black
D: Kitchen Cotton, Pumpkin
E: Wool Ease, Fisherman

Flower Cap, pages 36–37
A: Kitchen Cotton, Cayenne
B: Wool Ease, Blue Heather

I Heart You, pages 38–39
A: Jiffy, Caffe
B: Jiffy, Chili

Extraterrestrial, pages 40–41
A: Vanna's Choice, Sweet Pea
B: Vanna's Choice, Black

Antlers, pages 42–43
Jiffy, Caffe

Party Hat, pages 44–45
A: Vanna's Choice, Raspberry
B: Wool Ease, Fisherman
C: Vanna's Choice, Mint

Witch, pages 46–47
A: Kitchen Cotton, Grape
B: Kitchen Cotton, Snap Pea

Cupcake, pages 48–49
A: Vanna's Choice, Pink Poodle
B: Vanna's Choice, Berrylicious
C: Vanna's Choice, Angel White

Banana, pages 50–51
A: Baby's First, Honeybee
B: Wool Ease, Cocoa

Santa Hat, pages 52–55
A: Jiffy, Chili
B: Jiffy, White

Elf, pages 56–57
A: Jiffy, Apple
B: Jiffy, Chili

Top Hat, pages 58–61
A: Fun Yarn, Black
B: Vanna's Glamour, Moonstone

Pom Pom Hat, pages 62–63
A: Vanna's Choice, Raspberry
B: Vanna's Choice, Fern

Little Lion, pages 64–67
A: Vanna's Choice, Honey
B: Wool Ease, Paprika

Feline Fox, pages 68–71
A: Wool Ease, Paprika
B: Wool Ease, Fisherman
C: Fun Yarn, Black

Baby Bear, pages 72–75
A: Heartland Yarn, Big Bend
B: Wool Ease, Fisherman

Dog, pages 76–79
A: Wool Ease, Fisherman
B: Heartland Yarn, Big Bend

Shark Attack, pages 80–83
A: Kitchen Cotton, Tropic Breeze
B: Kitchen Cotton, Red
C: Kitchen Cotton, Vanilla

Santa Paws, pages 84–87
A: Vanna's Choice, Scarlet
B: Vanna's Choice, White

Candy Corn, pages 88–91
A: Kitchen Cotton, Citrus
B: Kitchen Cotton, Vanilla
C: Kitchen Cotton, Pumpkin

Unicorn, pages 92–95
A: Vanna's Choice, Dusty Purple
B: Vanna's Choice, Aqua

Cowboy Hat, pages 96–99
A: Vanna's Choice, Beige
B: Kitchen Cotton, Tropic Breeze
C: Wool Ease, Paprika

Made in the USA
Las Vegas, NV
29 November 2024